Teach your
PUPPY
to be the dog you want

Clarice Rutherford & David H. Neil

foulsha

LONDON • NEW YORK • TOI

CW00969890

foulsham

The Oriel, Thames Valley Court, 183–187 Bath Road,
Slough, Berkshire SL1 4AA, England

Foulsham books can be found in all good bookshops and direct from
www.foulsham.com

ISBN: 978-0-572-03491-7

Originally published as *How to Raise a Puppy You Can Live With*,
4th edition, 2005 by Alpine Publications, Inc., 38262 Linman Road,
Crawford, CO 81415, USA

This Anglicised edition published 2008 by W. Foulsham & Co. Ltd

Illustrations by Nancy Robinson, Julie Sorbie and Terry Nash

Cover photograph © Superstock

A CIP record for this book is available from the British Library

Printed and bound in the UK by CPI Mackays, Chatham ME5 8TD

CONTENTS

ACKNOWLEDGEMENTS

We wish to thank the people who have aided in the preparation of the fourth edition of this book: Barbara Fleming for organising the new text, Elizabeth Stimmel for typing the complete text, Deborah Helmers for her patient and thorough editing, Kelly Hines Keller for graphic design and Sue Henning for her continuing work on puppy temperament testing.

A CONTRACT

To all the puppy people who have made a choice ...

I have chosen to share my life with you, a member of another species.
I pledge to appreciate your uniqueness as a member of the canine family
and to attempt to raise you and discipline you in terms of this uniqueness.

In return, I know that you will do your best to fit into my lifestyle
if it is caninely possible, and will reciprocate my attention to you
by letting me share your view of the universe.

I will be a better person for having this experience.
I hope your life will be better for having lived with me.

ABOUT THE AUTHORS

Clarice Rutherford is co-author of *Retriever Puppy Training*. A Labrador breeder in past years, she is a member of breed and obedience clubs and has competed in breed, obedience and field events. Mrs Rutherford obtained a BS degree in Animal Science and an MS in English from Colorado State University and was employed for several years at the CSU Animal Care Center.

Through her work in obedience classes, she has seen too many dogs living lives of quiet desperation (or, more likely, noisy and hyperactive desperation) – very little stimulation in their environment and lack of consistency in the way their owners treat them. This results from the owners' lack of appreciation for what the dog has to offer. The dog is a victim of abuse because of the ignorance of people. We have domesticated the dog to the extent that he is totally dependent on humans – and then we abuse him by refusing to understand his needs in the sophisticated world of the twenty-first century. Mrs Rutherford's goal is to help people understand the nature of the dog they live with, respect his dogness, and, in return, be respected by their dog.

Dr David Neil received his veterinary degree from the University of Liverpool in the United Kingdom in 1959 and was in mixed private practice in Wales and then England for three years. During that time, he came to rely heavily on the almost uncanny ability of the working sheepdogs, particularly where the treatment of large flocks was involved. Throughout his career, many ethical questions brought him face to face with man's use of, and interactions with, domestic animals. He has been an active participant in the humane movement and was president of the Humane Society for Larimer County (Colorado) from 1978 to 1981. Currently, he is involved with the Canadian Federation of Humane Societies and the Alberta SPCA.

Since the first edition of this book was published in the U.S. in 1981, there has continued to be a great deal of activity in attempting to reduce the large number of unwanted dogs that regrettably must be euthanised each year. The authors remain committed to help deal with this problem by doing what they can to ensure that people end up with a dog they can live with and share much happiness together.

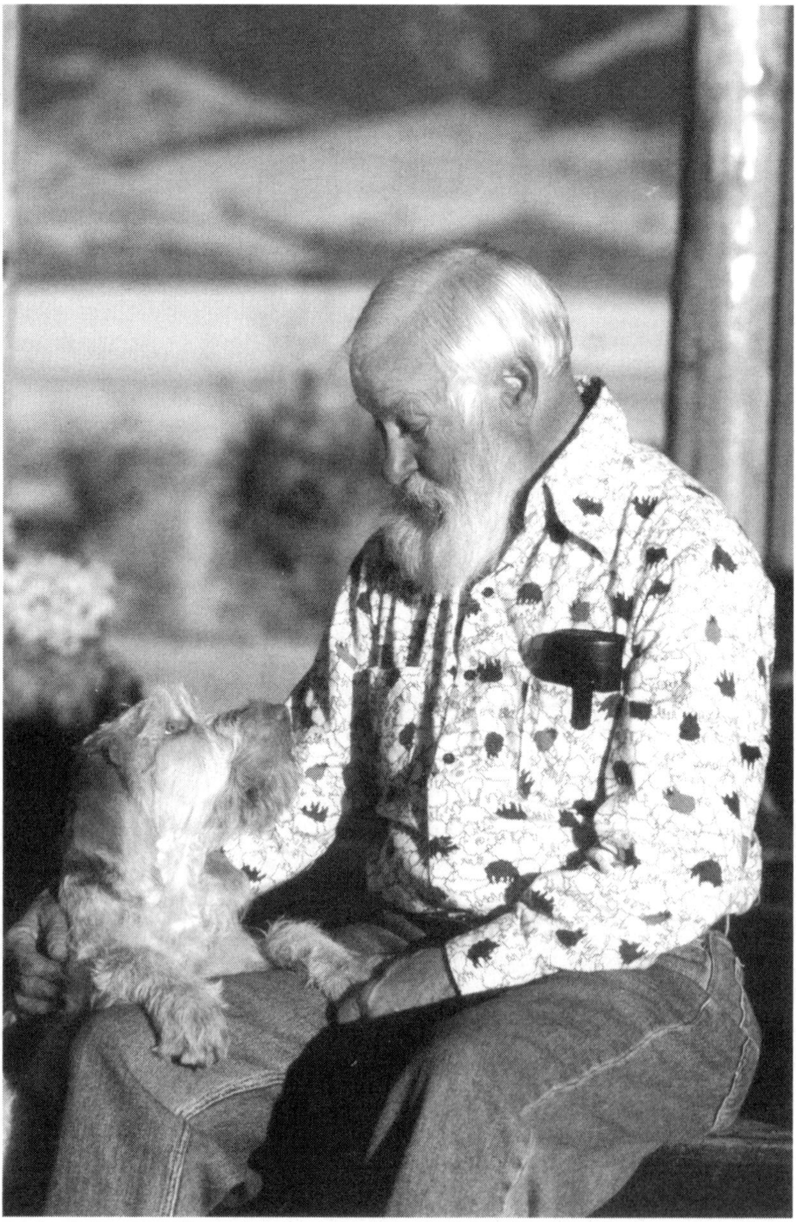

PHOTO © JUDITH STROM

Introduction

Every year, countless numbers of people develop relationships with their dogs in work and play, allowing subtle, effective two-way communication to be comfortably established. In some of these relationships, the bond continues to grow stronger, and what begins as a matter of expediency between two awkward strangers – the new owner and the new puppy dog – becomes, in the fullness of time, a meeting of minds and hearts.

At the dawn of civilisation in the ancient city of Jericho, there were dogs as large as wolves and as small as terriers. Already man had selected and bred different types of dogs for different functions. This selecting and breeding has continued for thousands of years as a continuous process. Today approximately 200 breeds are recognised by the Kennel Club, breeds which in one way or another enrich our lives in work and play. We see the amazing adaptation of various breeds to become guide dogs for the blind and deaf. Dogs also assist the physically handicapped. No matter what functions dogs perform, the basic, underlying theme throughout the vast majority of them is *companionship*. Pet dogs in contemporary society continue to provide a focus of attention and affection for people who feel very much alone, whether confined to their homes or to an institutional setting.

If the status quo prevails, dog ownership is going to get tougher, and deservedly so …
The way we play it may have a very significant impact on the future of the domestic dog in urban society.

However, having praised dogs to the skies, we recognise that all is not well with the unwritten contract between man and dog. Too many dogs do not enjoy a healthy family situation and get into so much trouble that they are either impounded or relinquished to the animal shelter. A high percentage of these animals are approximately 18 months old and, having outgrown their cuteness, are having behavioural problems that their owners could not deal with. Our purpose in writing this book is to help people understand their puppy's behaviours and needs as he grows into maturity.

We believe that the first step towards getting a dog that you and everyone else can live with – after selecting the right breed for you, of course – is to find a good breeder who recognises how important the first two months of a puppy's life are in determining how he will be able to deal with the big world as a mature dog. When your carefully selected puppy comes home with you, you are now in the driving seat, and your knowledge and patient actions will further determine whether you will soon own a dog that you – and your entire community – can live with.

One of the big issues involves raising a normal puppy when during the day the entire household is either out to work or at school. Recognising that separation anxiety is a serious problem, we have addressed this both in terms of proofing the puppy against the development of separation anxiety as well as recognising some of its signs and dealing with them when they start to occur in later months.

PHOTO © JUDITH STROM

Look for the puppy with the personality that most closely fits your ideal. Observe the puppies as a group, but don't make a decision based on the puppy's behaviour with the littermates. Take him away from the litter and evaluate his response to you as well.

CHAPTER 1

Choosing Your Puppy

When you visit a litter of little puppies that are so easy to handle and control, it is easy to overlook the thought that within a few months these puppies will have the size and general behavioural characteristics of their breed, together with the individual behavioural tendencies inherited from the parents. Unfortunately, when you select one of the puppies and take him home, you might be unhappy with the result, because that little puppy can change into a much larger and more vigorous dog than your home and lifestyle can manage. It isn't the puppy's fault if you didn't think about the adult dog that the puppy would become.

The best puppy for you is the one you can live with, and everyone else can, too. When choosing a puppy, you must be able to visualise what the adult dog will be like physically and behaviourally and how he will fit into your home facilities as well as into your life. For instance, a person who would be very content with a relatively slow-moving Basset would probably be frustrated with a quick-moving, high-energy terrier.

Perhaps the first deliberate action in acquiring a puppy is to set aside sufficient time to familiarise yourself with all that the world of dogs can offer you, and, in turn, what you can offer a dog. During this time, you can resort to the abundant literature on dogs and seek expert advice. In this way, you start to zero in on that special little chap that will so enrich your life in the future.

The best puppy for you is the one that will grow up into the right dog for you. When choosing a puppy, you must be able to visualise what the adult dog will be like, physically and behaviourally.

Don't pick a breed on its looks alone – you could be surprised.

A puppy's adult personality will be shaped by a combination of three factors – his breed, his individual genetic behaviour and the socialisation that he receives during the first four months of life. Breed characteristics are generalisations, of course, but they are recognisable in most members of each particular breed. It is obvious that different breeds not only look different but behave differently. Don't pick a breed on its looks alone – you could be surprised.

Selecting Based on Breed Characteristics

When you begin reading about the different breeds, note the history of each one. This informs you of the specific reasons for which they were bred and the purpose they served for their humans and gives you an idea of the built-in behaviour and attitude of those breeds.

Dogs are descended from the wolf, whom we know to be *a hunter, a herder* (directing his prey in a particular direction), *a guard* (protecting his food supply and his den of puppies), *a team player* (working together to run down prey), *an athlete* (loping across great distances) and *an aware animal* (having intensely acute senses of sight, scenting and hearing). Each of these qualities is called a *drive* or *instinct*.

All of the qualities we admire in the dog come from the prey drive of the wolf. This prey drive in the wolf is a combination of instincts that all fit together to guarantee survival of the pack: *the pack instinct, the prey instinct, the herding instinct, the guarding instinct* and *the communication instinct*. This collection of instincts in the dog translates into behaviours that can make him a welcome member of his human family. With the right training, he learns to live comfortably in his people group, his people pack. He knows not to bite. He communicates through body language, and he understands and practises non-verbal communication.

The wolf is a hunter. The prey instinct governs his life. He lives for his major reward, to chase the prey and kill it. The prey instinct is ever present, always turned on, ready to activate.

The dog *also* is a hunter. The prey instinct is in every breed, but to a milder degree than in the wolf. Many dogs that live sheltered lives seldom have an opportunity to display any prey instinct. But even for these dogs, certain sounds and movements can activate the instinct and cause the dog to react like a wolf. When we understand that this is part of the dog's behaviour and personality, we can help the family pack be a pleasant union of individuals who are different and yet respect and enjoy each other.

Understanding how the instincts occur in different breeds will help you to select the puppy that fits most comfortably in your family pack. The different breeds were selected to emphasise one or more of these drives, which then became part of the dog's personality. For example, the Collie, the Shetland

Sheepdog and the Corgi were bred for herding sheep and cattle, and you might find yours herding a group of children in your garden by circling around them. The northern breeds, such as Siberian Huskies, Samoyeds and Malamutes, were selected in their gene pool for pulling and going forwards continuously. Your Husky will need to be on a leash or he might decide to take off on a run. The purpose of the sporting breeds is to find game, with the retrievers specialising in returning the game to their person. You will find them picking up and carrying things around the house. The scent hounds have an intense scenting ability, and when they catch an interesting scent, they follow it regardless of what you say. But all these dogs still bond to their people. This is the basic difference between dogs and wolves.

HERD • PULL

Understanding how instincts are expressed in different breeds will help you to select a puppy that fits most comfortably in your family pack.

RETRIEVE • HUNT

The terriers, bred to hunt and catch small animals, are quick moving with high energy and are always ready for a chase. Working dogs such as German Shepherds and Rottweilers know that they have a job to do for their humans. They were expected to protect flocks from wolves, coyotes and mountain lions, as well as to protect their humans. Toy breeds were bred to be companion dogs and prefer spending time close to their humans.

When you select your own puppy, think about the characteristics that were bred into that particular breed, which of the drives are strongest, and what that tells you about the future behaviour of your dog. Try to be objective when you decide whether those characteristics will fit with your own personality. Think about the dog's need for exercise, his activity level in the house, his attitude towards visitors and his trainability.

PHOTO © JUDITH STROM

Sporting breeds are bred to scent and retrieve game.

PHOTO © JUDITH STROM

This West Highland White Terrier puppy is learning to have his feet wiped when he comes inside.

Once you have decided on your breed, you will find a range of personalities within that breed — some more quiet, others more dominant. You will look for the puppy that best fits the image you have for your canine companion.

Contact the Kennel Club for a list of Accredited Breeders and for details of Breed Clubs. The Kennel Club's website includes a Puppy Sales Register that lists breeders in all parts of the country. When buying a puppy, **you're not just buying a pedigree – you're buying the expertise**, the understanding of the puppy's needs and the advice that the breeder can give you based on experience with that particular breed.

You can also gain good information by attending a dog show and buying a catalogue of the dogs entered. This lists the names and addresses of the people who are showing, and you can follow up by contacting a breeder in your area. *Dog World, Your Dog* and *Dog Monthly*, found at many magazine stands, list breeders in all parts of the country.

When you contact a breeder, you will probably be asked questions about your lifestyle and about the plans that you have for your dog. Do you have enough time to give your dog? Good breeders want to be sure that the puppy goes to a good home.

We cannot recommend buying puppies that are born in puppy farms (and usually sold in pet shops). You cannot learn anything about the parents of the puppy and will know nothing about the treatment that the puppy received during the sensitive stages of birth to eight weeks nor about any hidden health problems.

When you have selected the breed that has a size and disposition best for you, it is time to consider the individual personality that you want your puppy to have. A good indication of this is the personality of the parent dogs. Behaviour is a hereditary factor, just as are the appearance, the length of coat or the type of head. Behaviour is of great importance to most buyers. Therefore, if either parent is very shy or very aggressive, you will want to look at other litters before making a choice. Conversely, if the parent dogs like people and are pleasant to be around, you will know that there is a good chance that the puppies will have the same qualities. The puppy will not be a carbon copy of either parent but will probably have some of the behavioural characteristics of each.

The third aspect of the development of a puppy's personality (after breed and heredity) is the socialising that he receives from the breeder and the

The puppy should have a good temperament if the sire and dam have good personalities and the litter has been properly socialised.

behaviour moulding that he receives from his new master. Every breeder knows that careful breeding is only part of the story, although a very important part. Breeders have seen promising puppies ruined by bad training or simply a lack of training, or by mismatching a puppy with a certain type of person. If a breeder tells you that he doesn't think a dog is right for you, he does so from experience based on placing puppies.

Choosing the Right Puppy

Selecting a puppy is often a matter of deciding which puppy is most likely to fit your personality. For example, if at seven and eight weeks of age a Labrador Retriever puppy is running around as fast as he can, grabbing your trouser leg, crashing into you when you're down on your knees, jumping up into your face or grabbing at your hand when you try to pet him, then you can be certain this puppy will be a handful. Another Labrador puppy in that same litter may be quiet, may come to you slowly at first and may lick your hand or face. This puppy will be easier to train and, because he's a Labrador, you know he will become sufficiently lively when he is acquainted with his new home. Which puppy is best for you? Perhaps you prefer a puppy that isn't always fussing for attention. An independent puppy that is busy sniffing, not caring whether he's petted, might develop into the type of dog you would want once you have bonded to each other.

Many breeders have puppies that are reserved ahead of time, with each person getting a pick in order. For example, you might have the third-pick female because two people reserved a puppy before you did. Another person might have fourth-pick male (if there are that many). It might seem that you won't get the puppy that's best for you, but the breeder often helps to match puppies and people, and it's amazing how the puppies seem to go to the most suitable homes. Many breeders use puppy testing and their own evaluations to match puppies and people. You can also use your own guidelines. See the Chapter on Puppy Temperament Testing (page 145).

Observation of a puppy with his littermates sometimes gives a false impression of the puppy's innate desire to please and to adjust to people. Never select a puppy based on his behaviour with his littermates. Remove him from the litter and play with him individually. Observations made by an inexperienced buyer on only one visit may not accurately reflect the true puppy – the hell-raiser might be tired, and the wallflower may have just awakened and may be feeling his oats. More than one observation, the breeder's opinions and testing will give a better rounded picture and may prevent a mismatch.

If you have the pick between two or three puppies, carry one puppy away from the litter, far enough so that the puppy can't see or hear his littermates. Is the puppy curious, wagging his tail and exploring? Is he worried and trying to return to the litter? Can you attract his attention by clapping your hands, or by bending down close to him and having him run to you? Does he follow you when you walk past and coax him? Does the puppy look at you when you hold him close and talk to him? Roll the puppy on his back and hold him gently. Read the score sheet on page 156 to evaluate his reaction. The final decision on your part might be an emotional one, but part of that selection process is based on how you react to the puppy on a one-to-one basis. The puppy that you don't want is the shy puppy that wants to run and hide or the aggressive puppy that nips at you when you try to play with him.

PHOTO © JUDITH STROM

React to a puppy on a one-to-one basis.

When You Can't Visit the Litter

You will have to trust the breeder if you can't visit the litter. Ask all the questions you can think of. Tell the breeder the type of puppy you want, then rely on the breeder to make the final decision. Many breeders require a deposit if you want a puppy held for you. The remaining payment is made when you pick up the puppy, or just before shipping. You should receive the puppy litter registration at this time or a written promise that it soon will be in the post.

Deciding on the Best Age

Many breeders consider nine weeks to be the ideal age for a puppy to leave his littermates and go to his new home. Others prefer to keep their puppies in the litter until ten weeks of age. A licensed breeder is guilty of an offence if he sells a dog that is less than eight weeks of age and no reputable unlicensed dealer will sell a puppy that is younger than eight weeks. The Live Animals Regulations prohibit air transport of puppies under eight weeks of age. It is advisable for the buyer to be guided by the experience of the breeder. **The main concern for the new owner is to be certain that the puppy has received sufficient individual attention and puppy training from the breeder.**

The Older Puppy

If you are considering a puppy that is 12 weeks or older, you need to get two assurances from the breeder. First, the puppy must have been taken out of his pen on a regular basis to experience different environments; otherwise, kennel shyness may develop. Second, the puppy must have spent time alone with a person on a regular basis (for example,15 minutes a day, four or five days a week); if not, his socialisation will be retarded, and much time and effort will be necessary to bring the puppy around to a normal attitude towards people and other dogs. If these two aspects have been taken care of by the breeder – in other words, **if the puppy training has begun – you will be fine buying an older puppy.**

Don't Take Home Two

If you want two puppies, wait until the first puppy is five to six months old before bringing home the second. By this time, the puppy will have bonded to you and will be comfortable spending more time alone in his garden or house area. The problem with littermates is that the initial bonding is to each other rather than to you. If they have each other, neither puppy will give you his full attention. This makes training almost impossible. Contemporary research in dog behaviour indicates that puppy–human bonding is essential to a superior relationship. **It's a very rare person who can induce bonding with more than one puppy at a time.**

Other Considerations

Unfortunately, some individuals raise puppies only for what financial gain they might experience, and they care nothing about the needs of the puppies. **Don't hesitate to ask for specific information.** Get a detailed report of what care and activities have been done with the puppies, and find out how knowledgeable the person is about the characteristics and history of the breed. If the breeder seems lacking in any of these areas, don't fall victim to a hard sell. These people should not be encouraged to perpetuate their puppy activities. They do more harm than good for the dog world.

> *Don't hesitate to ask for specifics about your puppy – a good breeder will share with you all the litter details you request.*

There are many conscientious and reliable breeders who breed and raise puppies with great care. **Take the time to find the right one.** A good breeder will tell you why she did this particular breeding and will share with you her expectations for the litter.

We have the advantage of raising and training dogs in a time when much has been discovered about the basic developmental periods of a puppy's life. This is very exciting. We can take what heredity gives us and then control the environment to develop the best possible personality in the adult dog.

PHOTO © MEGGIN RUTHERFORD

Often a puppy will pick you and bond very quickly. If your other criteria are met by this individual, he may be the right choice.

CHAPTER 2

Behaviour: Environmental Factors

A major portion of this book pertains to the first six months of a puppy's life, with emphasis on the first three months. There's a good reason for this. We believe that these early months are absolutely the key to moulding a dog's behaviour so that he can fit into the complexities of life in the twenty-first century. Let's face it, urban life isn't exactly a natural environment for man's best friend – but with care it can be one to which he can adapt.

Life was great for the dog in the days when the family dog went everywhere with the childen and also had his own circle of friends among the other dogs in the neighbourhood. In contrast, today most dogs live isolated lives in gardens, pens or homes, completely at the mercy of a few members of the family who are often very busy with other activities. If the dog is fed every day and has shelter, we are too likely to think that we're fulfilling his needs.

The dog is, by virtue of his wolf heritage, a pack animal with definite social needs. Through the millennia while man and dog were evolving, the dog developed empathy with humans and a desire for attention from his human pack members. If this need for attention is ignored, the dog can become very frustrated and might well begin to indulge in activities like incessant barking and destroying property. If the dog that is kept in such an environment as an adult also was bred and raised with inadequate attention, the problem is compounded.

*Urban living does not come naturally to a dog,
but by understanding a puppy's needs
we can help him to adjust.*

Environment Shapes Behaviour

Dog behaviour studies have determined that the first 12 weeks of a dog's life are vitally important because a puppy's experiences during this time will affect his emotional responses as an adult dog. It stands to reason, then, that if we know how the puppy is growing and what he needs during these different stages, we can help every puppy get the best possible start in life.

The need for human attention begins shortly after the puppy is born. During the first few weeks of life, the puppy is going through the most amazing process of growth. At first, his world is dark and silent and consists solely of contact with his littermates and the constant care of his mother. After about two weeks he begins to learn new behaviours that will adapt him well to living in a sensory and social world. By eight weeks of age he has full use of his sensory and motor systems, and his central nervous system has reached maturity, ready for whatever learning experiences await.

PHOTO © JAMES DIGBY

At about two weeks of age the puppy begins learning new behaviours that help him adapt to living in a social world.

The puppy's central nervous system, and therefore his behaviour, develops in a wondrously particular and precise pattern, and each stage of growth has an effect on the puppy's actions. If the puppy doesn't have his physical and social needs satisfied during any one of these periods, certain characteristics of his personality will be stalled at that particular stage of development. This, in turn, will have an effect on how the dog will behave when he is older.

For example, some dogs remain overly suspicious of anything new or different, often because they never developed investigative behaviour when it was a normal part of their growing up (eight to 12 weeks). Another dog might be too easily excited, to the extent of appearing hyperactive, as a result of not having had adequate environmental stimulation during the stage of learning how to sort out sound, sight and smells (six to ten weeks). And both the shy and the hyperactive personality can be strongly affected by a lack of human contact from three to seven weeks.

You are undoubtedly wondering if knowing about these developmental stages in a puppy's life is all that important. Obviously, many dog owners have raised very fine dogs without such information – for good reasons. These puppies may have had outgoing personalities and been able to overcome some lack of socialisation. Even more likely, these puppies were fortunate enough to be raised in homes where their needs were automatically and unknowingly met during each period. After all, dogs have been successfully socialised for more than 10,000 years without anyone being specifically aware of it, let alone labelling the process!

Dogs have been successfully socialised for over 10,000 years, without much instruction.

With a little encouragement, your puppy will grow up healthy and well-adjusted!

So it is today in many homes. Puppies that get a lot of attention and receive touch, sound and visual stimulation in the course of a normal day grow up to be healthy, well-adjusted dogs.

The Breeder's Role Is Foremost

Beginning with the breeder, a certain amount of time must be reserved for puppy activities. This is why timing the arrival of a litter is important. A concerned breeder checks the calendar when planning a breeding to make sure that puppies will not be neglected. If certain social obligations or an unusually heavy workload will occur at a particular time of the year, a litter should not be bred to arrive at such a time.

The breeder who is not willing to give some time to the puppies should let someone else do breeding and puppy raising. There are enough poorly adjusted dogs in the world now that did not get the people-care they needed while they were puppies.

This is where the so-called 'puppy farms' are totally negligent. The people who operate these farms have a large number of female dogs whose only function is to produce puppies for profit and that are often kept isolated in cages, boxes or other very small areas. This so-called 'breeder' has no understanding of the needs of the dog and does not realise the damage done to a puppy's personality by giving him no socialisation during the first eight weeks. It is not only extreme cruelty to keep the parent dogs in such confining isolation, but it is also cruel to the puppies to deny them the socialisation they must have if they are to adjust to living with people as they grow up.

PHOTO © MEGGIN RUTHERFORD

The breeder is teaching this young puppy to come for a treat.

Today, so much has been learnt about dog behaviour that there is no excuse for a socially maladjusted dog. Whether you are a breeder who is introducing the world of dogs to newcomers, or whether you are a first-time puppy owner, there is much you can do to make this a good world for your pet. You may not have the luxury of many days and weeks to be a partner in your puppy's personality development. But you don't have to give up a normal routine and become a 'puppy-recluse' in order to accomplish your goal. Mostly, you just need to be aware of what's going on in the natural process as a newborn puppy grows from a 'blob' into a bouncing young adult.

CHAPTER 3

The First Three Months

The first three months of a dog's life are called the *developmental months* because it is during this time that almost all of the dog's basic behavioural patterns are developed. At least the first eight weeks of the puppy's life are the responsibility of the breeder. Beyond that age, the responsibility for socialisation shifts to the new owner. Each period has specific activities that can help a puppy to grow emotionally.

The Developmental Periods

There are three basic developmental periods in the first 12 weeks. These periods are defined here by calendar time, but this doesn't mean that all puppies will begin each period on exactly the same day. There will be variances depending upon the breed and upon individual differences within the litter. Littermates usually catch up with each other, however, by the end of the last period.

> *Experiences during the first three months are the foundation of the puppy's mature personality.*

Basic Developmental Periods

Neonatal Period	Transitional Period	Socialisation Period
Days 1–14	Days 15–21	Days 22–84
Birth to two weeks	Two to three weeks	Three to 12 weeks

In order for us to understand a puppy's needs as he begins to grow, we should become familiar with the characteristics of the different periods. This chapter will cover the general description of each period. Chapter 4 will discuss the breeder's role in raising puppies, and Chapters 5 and 6 will deal with the new owner's activities in taking a puppy to his new home.

The Neonatal Period

Days 1–14   **Key Puppy Behaviour:**

Spends 90 per cent of time sleeping

Is susceptible to excess heat or cold

Crawls

Nurses

Seeks warmth of littermates and mother

Can usually right himself if turned over

Needs stimulation for urination and defecation

During the neonatal period, the bitch is the main influence on the puppy. Her health, milk supply and attitude towards the puppies and later towards people who come to look at the puppies will influence the behavioural development of the litter. If she is overly fearful or aggressive, this can be imprinted on the puppies, and their future behaviour might be very similar to hers, whether or not they were born with a fearful or aggressive genetic trait. Thus, a behaviour can be either genetically or environmentally derived.

A puppy's behaviour can be both genetically and environmentally derived.

At this age, the puppy's abilities are confined to sucking, vocalising and crawling slowly. The senses of sight and hearing are not functional yet. The eyes may begin to open around ten days of age but in most cases are not open until about 14 days of age.

The puppy learns about his environment through touch. You can observe him crawling around, moving his head from side to side until he bumps into his mother or a littermate. A puppy might crawl away from the bitch, but she should be able to retrieve him by carrying him in her mouth, providing he doesn't crawl out of her sight or sound. Urination and defecation are reflex responses that occur only when the bitch licks her puppies' anal and genital regions.

PHOTO © THE ALASKAN MALAMUTE BY BROOKS AND WALLACE

The bitch's attitude will affect the behaviour of the puppies.

During this neonatal period, the puppy is aware only of heat, cold and pain. He is not yet capable of regulating body heat efficiently and therefore needs his mother and the other puppies to help maintain his own warmth. Even though it looks as though the puppies do nothing but eat and sleep, this is a very important period. The central nervous system is rapidly developing, getting ready for the next stage.

The Transitional Period

Days 15–21   **Key Puppy Behaviour:**

Eyes open

Teeth begin to emerge

Stands on all fours and take a few steps

Begins to lap liquid

Defecates without the bitch's stimulation

The puppy's eyesight is dim, but he is ready for the next adventure. He discovers that the other puppies are more than just warm lumps to be crawled over and slept on. He begins to stagger around on four legs, lifting himself up first on his front legs, then on his hind legs as they become equally strong. Activity periods are brief, followed by sleep to gather strength for the next concentrated effort. By the end of this transitional period, the puppy can walk on four legs and lap milk or soft food in a fairly efficient manner (although not very elegantly).

As soon as their eyes open, the puppies will begin to explore their environment.

The puppy no longer needs constant care from the bitch and is beginning to defecate without her stimulus. He starts to get interested in littermates. The very beginnings of pack-oriented behaviour, such as pawing at each other's faces and chewing on littermates' ears, are seen at this stage.

The Socialisation Period

Socialisation is the name given to the next nine weeks, the growth period lasting from three to 12 weeks of age. We have found that this period can be divided into four stages, each of which is an important stepping stone for the one that follows.

The dog's primary social relationships develop during this time. If his primary relationships are with people, the puppy will be able to form lasting relationships throughout his life, but the puppy that receives little human contact during this time will find it difficult to adjust to humans as long as he lives.

The puppy also needs to be with littermates and the bitch during the first weeks of the socialisation period. He needs to learn how to act around other members of his own species, or he could become a dog that picks fights easily or has problems with mating (if this should subsequently be desired).

We have divided the socialisation period into four stages not only for ease of discussion but also because the behavioural patterns of the puppy are readily distinguishable and determined by their physical age.

First Stage – The Period of Becoming Aware

Days 22–35	Key Puppy Behaviour:
3–4 weeks	Can hear, see and the sense of smell is becoming much more complex
	Begins to eat food
	Begins to bark, wag tail and bite other puppies
4–5 weeks	Uses legs quite well, but tires easily
	Paws
	Bares teeth and growls
	Chases
	Plays prey-killing games

The beginning of the socialisation period can be determined for each puppy by using the startle-reaction test. When a puppy visibly reacts to a loud sound, he is into the socialisation stage. This is also a means of telling which puppies are on a slightly different time schedule in their physical development. This is valuable information because otherwise these puppies might unjustly be labelled as dull-witted or slow when actually the only problem is that they need time to catch up physically with the others. Puppies don't always go by the book and react on the 21st or 22nd day. One breeder accidentally dropped a pan about a metre from his puppies on the 18th day and got a big reaction, while on the 21st day the puppies didn't react to a loud noise. By then they apparently accepted it as part of their world.

Even if we didn't look at the calendar or use the startle test, we would know when the socialisation period begins. It's as if someone pushed the 'on' button. Virtually overnight, the puppy turns into an animated little being. The central nervous system continues to develop rapidly during this time. The puppy now has both sight and hearing ability and by four weeks is beginning to develop perception of distance. The sense of smell, which is one of the first senses to develop, is now starting to develop the subtlety that is such an important part of the adult dog's perception of the world.

From 22 to 28 days, the puppy is experiencing a shower of sensory stimulation. So much awareness of the world around him is developing so quickly that the puppy needs a very stable home environment to balance the excess stimulation. The bitch should remain with the litter as much as possible during this week.

By the end of the third week, the puppy displays much more complex behaviour than at the beginning of the period, which is an indication of how rapidly development occurs. The puppies now play together. They start to learn how much chewing and biting the other puppies will take. They begin to show adult behaviour patterns with their play-fighting, scruff-holding and prey-killing (head-shaking) movements, and they are beginning to bark, growl and snap at each other. Some puppies begin barking and wagging tails around three weeks of age, but this varies with the breed and the individuals.

Let your puppy enjoy moving through this stage ...or you might end up with a 'perpetual puppy'.

It is possible for many a puppy's behavioural patterns to get stalled at this stage because he isn't allowed to act normally during the next two periods. This occurs especially among the toy breeds because of attitudes towards their size, but it can happen with any breed. When a puppy is not ever allowed to act like a dog (e.g., rough-and-tumble playing with other puppies, investigating all corners of this world), never experiences stress of any kind and has all his needs met before they even arise, he becomes a spoiled pet – a perpetual puppy. The breeder is cheating the dog by not allowing him to develop into a mature canid, and the owner is cheating himself of the pleasure of having a mature dog as a companion.

PHOTO © JAMES DIGBY

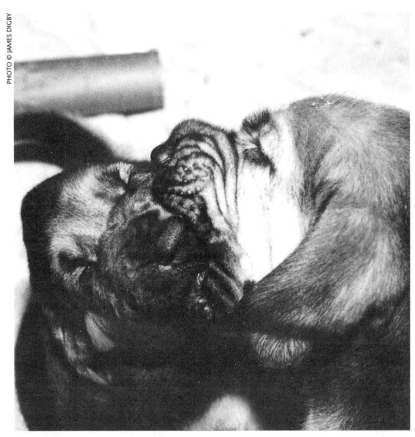

Puppies learn bite inhibition from each other; if one bites too hard, he soon suffers the consequences.

By the end of the third week, the puppies begin to play together and with their mother. The bitch can be separated from her puppies for short periods during the day, but her presence is still very important to their development.

Second Stage — The Period of Curiosity

Days 36–49   **Key Puppy Behaviour:**

5–7 weeks   Weaning begins

Is curious

Has little sense of fear

Participates in group activities and sexual play

Dominance order begins

This is an **extremely important** time in the puppy's life. It is the period when the puppy is totally dependent on the environment that you provide for him to stimulate and develop his genetic qualities. In addition to needing a stimulating environment, the puppy must receive attention from people. The kinds of experiences that a puppy has during this period have a very strong effect on how he will react emotionally to humans when he is an adult. If he has little contact with people except for being fed, he's probably not going to find it easy to accept human attention when he's older.

This is another time of rapid growth and change. During this period, a puppy acquires full use of his eyes and ears, his legs become stronger and more co-ordinated, and his brain reaches a final stage of physical development. Further development now largely depends on the experiences encountered by the otherwise fully equipped puppy.

PHOTO © JUDITH STROM

Dominance behaviour begins during this period.

At the beginning of this period, the puppy still has little sense of fear and is quick to approach anything and anybody. But by the end of these two weeks, he begins to be more cautious in his approach, which is all a part of learning to discriminate among sights, sounds and smells. Pups that don't go through these two periods of learning (having been isolated or overprotected) tend to become hyperactive adults. They have not learnt how to sort out sights, sounds and smells during these weeks and to identify the significant ones.

Sexual play is evident at this age. Mounting is quite common among male puppies, and sometimes females mount other puppies. This is a normal part of puppy play and is important in teaching puppies the normal sexual response as they mature. While mature males tend generally to confine their mounting to females, mounting to signify dominance over another male continues in maturity. Females also sometimes mount other females as a demonstration of dominance.

Many behaviourists agree that socialisation reaches a peak by the 49th day. From here on, human relationships, though still very important, begin to have a decreasing effect on the socialisation of the puppy. In other words, the amount of individual attention that a puppy has received by the 49th day can never be made up without a proportionally larger expenditure of time and effort.

From eight to ten weeks is considered by many breeders to be the right age for a puppy to go to his new home. By then the puppy has had sufficient time with his littermates for developing adequate dog behavioural patterns. His new owner can easily become the pack leader and can give the puppy individual attention and a lot of environmental variety. It is still essential, however, that opportunities for socialising with other dogs be made available on a regular basis. This ensures that the balance is maintained in interactions with other people and with dogs in the community.

Third Stage – The Period of Behavioural Refinement

Days 50–63	Key Puppy Behaviour:	
7–9 weeks	7 weeks:	Has total hearing and visual capacity Will investigate anything
	8 weeks:	Is fearful of sudden or loud sounds and movement Is cautious of anything new in the environment

The period of behavioural refinement is characterised by progression from unfettered curiosity to a more nervous evaluation of the stimulus created by the puppy's environment. This reaches its height around eight weeks of age and persists to about ten weeks of age.

This stage is an important milestone in a puppy's life. He reaches full visual and hearing capacity, and his brain is physically mature. This means that the brain is ready to perform its physical processes and the puppy can start learning to respond to your wishes as long as the learning process is taking place in very small steps. However, this doesn't mean that he's ready to be treated as an adult dog. He is still emotionally very immature.

This age is sometimes termed the 'fear period' because the puppy is very susceptible to long-lasting effects if he receives a bad fright during this time. At five and six weeks, a puppy can be severely frightened and in a relatively short period of time bounce back to his normal, happy self again. However, during the eighth week, if the puppy receives a bad fright, it may take weeks for him to return to his normal behaviour in the same frightening situation. He may even carry the fear all his life. A loud, rough person, a spanking, or an abnormally sharp noise are examples of frights that can cause such a reaction. Thus, shipping a puppy

Although this has been labelled the 'fear period', it's important to allow your puppy to have normal experiences.

to a new home by air freight during the eighth week could have a lasting bad effect. But don't think that you have to go to the other extreme and be overly protective, keeping your puppy in seclusion. Let him have normal experiences.

Puppies at this age also become hesitant about new and different objects and situations. During the preceding period (five to seven weeks), the puppy usually approached the unfamiliar fearlessly. Now, at eight weeks, the puppy is noticeably more hesitant in his approach. He may go back again and again to the same area or object as though he doesn't trust his initial judgement.

PHOTO © KENT AND DONNA DANNEN

Natural behaviours that occur between dogs should not be directed towards children or other family members.

An example of this caution is seen with retrievers – the five- to seven-week-old puppy will splash in shallow water or happily bounce into heavy grass, catkins or whatever is in his path. But during his eighth week, this same puppy will start to be suspicious of water, even a shallow pond, or a pile of rocks, and he seems to think that diving into a patch of weeds is unthinkable, at least not without a lot of sniffing and investigating first. However, by the end of the ninth week, this very puppy is returning to his previous crash-bang self.

This is all another normal and important part of the socialising process, a continuation of sorting out the multitude of smells, sounds and sights to determine what is important.

Fourth Stage – The Period of Environmental Awareness

Days 64–84   **Key Puppy Behaviour:**

9–12 weeks   Develops strong dominant and
                        subordinate behaviour among littermates

                    Begins to learn right behaviour for right circumstance

                    Continues to improve in motor skills

                    Has very short attention span

Even though no new behavioural patterns are evident during these weeks, the puppy is beginning to learn the right behaviours for the right times. This is no small task, and it is a necessary stage for the puppy to go through in the maturing process. His brain is ready for full functioning, but information must be fed into it one step at a time. It takes a puppy a long time to learn the acceptable ways of the world. This age is the culmination of the socialisation process. Exposure to different environments (as discussed in Chapter 6) is the primary consideration here.

Up to this age, the puppy has been very self-oriented. Most of his learning has been 'me'-directed. He has learnt to like his new family. He knows where his bed is, where the food is kept, where there's a warm place for a nap and (very importantly) where the urinating and defecating areas are. Now he's beginning to pay attention to you.

In fact, he thinks you're wonderful! He'll quickly learn his name. He'll come flying to you when you call him and get his attention. At this age, the puppy has a strong desire to please. After all, you're his whole world, having taken the place of mother and littermates.

The puppy pays attention to you, but he's also extremely busy learning everything he can about the world around him. The puppy's brain tissue reached its full physiological growth around eight weeks of age, and now he's ready to learn, to have experiences that will teach him how to behave, how to act like a dog, how to please a human – quite a challenge for the puppy, but one that he's ready for.

By ten weeks of age, strong dominant and subordinate behaviour is displayed among littermates. In some cases, this behaviour has been evident for three to four weeks. Any puppies remaining from the litter should start receiving individual attention and should receive their own special time alone with the breeder or other individual. Otherwise, the puppies will begin bonding with each other, will lose their interest in people and will become more difficult to train.

The last stage of socialisation is a most delightful one. At the same time that you should be actively moulding your puppy's behaviour (he won't always be this small and eager to please), you should also be enjoying your puppy. Relax and have fun. A puppy stays little such a short time – he'll be grown up before you know it.

PHOTO © JUDITH STROM

By nine weeks of age, puppies are busy learning about the world around them.

Developmental Periods of the First Three Months

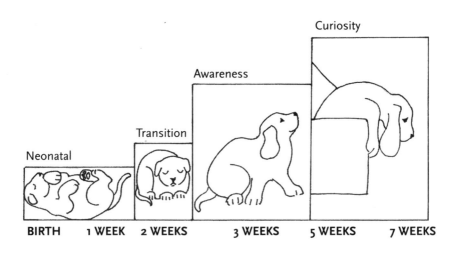

Curiosity

Awareness

Transition

Neonatal

| BIRTH | 1 WEEK | 2 WEEKS | 3 WEEKS | 5 WEEKS | 7 WEEKS |

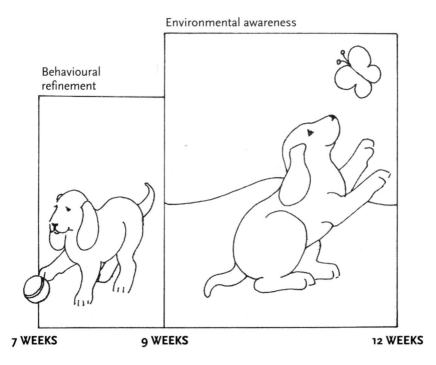

Environmental awareness

Behavioural refinement

| 7 WEEKS | 9 WEEKS | 12 WEEKS |

Summary of Puppy Behaviour
– What to Expect...

Weeks 1–2	All activities are innate: sucking, crying, crawling and touching. No sense of sight or sound. Susceptible to cold or heat. Must receive touching from bitch to stimulate elimination.
Week 3	Eyesight and hearing dim but rapidly improving. Begins to walk briefly. Interested in littermates. Begins eating and drinking and eliminates without stimulation from bitch.
Week 4	Needs stable environment. Becomes aware of a multitude of sights and sounds. Learns that people are important. Should remain with bitch as much as possible.
Week 5	Life has become exciting! Is not afraid. Becomes very aware of people and likes to be with them.
Week 6	Has full use of eyes and ears. Legs are stronger and more co-ordinated. Investigates everything in sight.
Week 7	Very involved in his own needs. Seldom responds to name. (You must take the initiative if you want him to follow you.) Can be started on house-training routine.
Week 8	Occasionally responds to name. Hesitant about approaching new things. Needs to take his own time when encountering new experiences.
Week 9	Will follow for short distance. Likes to lie beside or on top of your feet.
Weeks 10–12	Usually responds to name and comes when called from short distance. Will come when he hears the food dish rattle. Learns to avoid being stepped on. More dependable with house-training.

CHAPTER 4

The Breeder's Responsibility

Being a breeder of puppies is an important job – one that should be undertaken with a commitment for the time and effort necessary to get the puppies off to the best possible start. Aside from a clean, warm box area and good diet, a young puppy has definite behavioural needs. The breeder is the person who supplies these needs. During the first seven weeks, a puppy's three most important needs are **exposure to mild stress, a stimulating environment** and **individual attention**.

Exposure to Mild Stress

Even though the bitch is the primary influence in the puppy's life for the first 21 days, the breeder can at this time begin to influence a puppy's future behaviour. Although the puppy's eyes don't open until the end of the second week and his hearing isn't functioning until the third week, he will respond on a purely physical level to being touched. Touching and lifting the puppy begins to condition his physiology to react, at a very low level, to changes in his experience.

*A puppy's most important behavioural needs
during his first seven weeks are
exposure to mild stress, a stimulating environment
and individual attention.*

Principal Guidelines for Breeders

1. Plan a litter when you are able to provide the time and facilities necessary for proper socialisation and care.

2. Select breeding stock with sound, well-adjusted personalities from a line of dogs with good temperament.

3. Temperament-test the litter at seven weeks of age.

4. Cull from your breeding programme any dogs that produce poor temperament such as shyness, aggression or nervousness in their puppies. Also cull any dogs that exhibit bad behavioural traits that puppies may learn from association, such as barking and growling at people.

5. Spend at least five minutes every other day handling each puppy during the critical stage of five to seven weeks.

6. Provide stimulating facilities and toys for the litter. Introduce each puppy to a variety of environments before he leaves for his new home.

7. During the eighth week, make sure that the puppy is protected from loud sounds or sudden movements, which can create a fear that will take much time and effort to overcome.

8. Educate your puppy buyers in the proper socialisation, training and handling of the puppy, and try to assure yourself that the buyer is interested enough to put in the time for this training and socialisation before you sign the sales contract.

9. Follow up with your puppy buyers, and help them resolve behavioural problems at the onset.

10. Maintain contact with puppy buyers to determine how the puppies mature into adult dogs. Correlate this information with your notes on individual puppy temperaments. With experience, you will refine your ability to predict your puppies' temperament.

The First Two Weeks

Breeders who have made a practice of handling puppies at a very young age have observed that these puppies become very outgoing and confident as they get older. A study by Dr Michael Fox verifies and expands this observation. After conducting a study on the heart rates of puppies, he concluded that mildly stressing puppies will develop dogs that are superior when put in learning or competitive situations. Puppies that are handled at an early age and exposed to mild stress on a physiological level are better able to handle stress later in their lives without becoming emotionally disturbed or indulging in hyperactive behaviour. As a result, they learn quickly and are more responsive to new experiences in different environments.

Dr Carmen Battaglia, in his article 'Developing High Achievers', tells of a method developed by the U.S. military to improve the performance of dogs used for military service. It is termed the BioSensor Method, known to the public as the Super Dog Program. Based on research, the military studies confirmed that there are specific periods of time when neurological stimulation has important

During their first two weeks, puppies can benefit from brief, mild stimulation.

PHOTO © JAMES DIGBY

effects. The first period is a window of time between three days and 16 days during which there is rapid neurological development. Simple exercises at this time affect the neurological system by pushing it into action earlier than would happen normally, resulting in an increased capacity for future learning. Benefits include improved cardiovascular performance, greater resistance to stress and greater resistance to disease.

You can simulate these exercises with your own puppies. Pick up each puppy every day. Rub his softness against your cheek, and admire his miniature perfection – these are the fringe benefits. Hold him for about a minute, with the puppy's body firmly supported by your hand under his tummy. Weigh him if you desire. Using both hands, hold the puppy in an upright position, then in a head-down position and finally on his back, cradled in your hand. Touch a foot.

Don't pick up the puppies any more during the day, unless necessary of course. Children should not hold puppies at this age. Too much stress has a negative effect on the puppies' development.

Weeks Three to Seven

During these weeks, activities involve the senses and are stressful in the sense that these are new stimulations to the puppies. In the third week, pick the puppy up and use your thumb and finger to put light pressure on the ear or the foot. If he squeaks, he should calm quickly. For these puppies, repeat by touching, with no pressure at all, and progress to a slight pressure the next day.

The fourth week, 22 to 28 days, is a very stimulating one for the puppy. He is aware of the many sights and sounds around him and is quite excitable. About midway during the week, take the puppy away from his littermates and put him on a different floor surface than he has experienced before. As well as being a stress activity for the puppy, this is also valuable for observation of the puppy's behaviour and doesn't take more than three to four minutes per puppy.

Put the puppy down on cement, wood, dirt or fine gravel or linoleum if it isn't too slick for walking. If the area is bare, place a jacket on the floor, or place a chair or anything that represents a different object for the puppy to either approach or ignore. After you have put the puppy down on the floor, begin to record how he reacts to being alone, how quickly he begins to cry, whether he walks around or stays in one place, or if he investigates with his tail wagging.

It is easy to note extreme behaviours, but also take note of the 'even tempers'.

You can already begin to see differences in personality in the litter, and it is interesting to keep a record of these. Make a note of which puppies are the most aggressive feeders and which ones lose out in competition and always seem to end up on the outside of the puppy pile. Which puppies are the noisiest? Which ones squirm and cry when picked up, and which ones settle down and enjoy it?

The most extreme behaviours stand out first, of course, but don't forget to notice the puppies that are in the middle range of temperament. These are the puppies that will probably be easily trained as they grow older. Infrequently, it can happen that a puppy will show signs of brain damage, such as being able to move only in a tight circle. If you observe unusual behaviour, consult your vet about the severity of your particular case.

If the litter is large and the same colour, a dot of nail polish in different areas on the puppies or a collar of different-coloured rickrack helps to identify them as individuals.

During the fifth and sixth weeks, give the puppies mild auditory and visual stress. On one day during each week, play a radio for a few minutes near the

PHOTO © GLENDA JACKSON

In warm weather, puppies love exploring (and sleeping on!) grassy areas.

puppies when the puppies are awake. Play it at a loud but not blaring level. If you have normal hearing and it sounds loud but not irritating to you, it will be sufficient. On another day, give the puppies mild visual stress by flicking the room lights (not in bright daylight) for two or three minutes.

By the fifth week, individual attention by the breeder will become one of the mild stress activities because a small level of stress exists each time the puppy is removed from his littermates and taken to a different area where you are the main focus of his attention. Many puppies show no evidence of stress; others will be hesitant but will become more confident with each experience.

Puppies need socialising with friends and family.

Individual Attention

The interaction of the puppies with the bitch and with littermates is profoundly important for at least the first five weeks. If you want a puppy that is well adjusted to his identity as a canid, then his relationships with other dogs are very important. For example, the puppy learns from his littermates and his mother just how much of a bite is too much. He learns through this experience that he must control the use of his jaws.

As the puppy approaches the age of five weeks, the period of curiosity, he begins to explore and will leave his mother and his littermates at times. Among wild canids, other adult members of the pack would interact with the puppy, but with the domestic dog, this is the point at which people begin to take over the role of the canine mother, virtually reliving history and in so doing reinforcing the domestication of the puppy into the human world.

Time spent alone with each puppy helps him to learn that the name of the game is to be with people and to pay attention to people. Personal attention helps the puppy to develop a feeling of his importance as an individual. This in turn helps him to grow into a happy dog, eager to please his owner. One-on-one time with a puppy opens the second window of limited opportunity – socialisation. This period of time is between the fourth and 16th weeks of age. Lack of socialisation during these weeks inhibits the puppy's social and psychological development.

By the fifth week, 29 to 35 days, the central nervous system has developed substantially, and the puppies now have sight, hearing and smell (or scent) and are beginning to develop distance perception. However, even though the puppies need the stimulation of people, sights and sounds, emotionally they are still very immature and they tire easily; therefore, a little attention goes a long way. At least once during this week, but preferably twice, each puppy should be taken away from the puppy-pen area for at least five minutes. The time can be spent

Handle each puppy individually. Unthreatening eye contact and a warm facial expression offer a more intimate interaction with the puppy.

with informal play. Bend down so that your face is close to him, allowing you to interact on your puppy's level. Eye contact and facial expression offer a more intimate interaction.

This is a good age for new people and children to play with the puppies, provided caution is taken to see that the puppies aren't overstimulated. In fact, if there are no children in the home, invite children to visit the puppies.

During the sixth week, 36 to 42 days, it would be very unfortunate if the breeder neglected to see that each puppy got individual attention. People who visit the puppies can help. In the fifth week, the puppies probably weren't too interested in a person, but now, at six weeks, most puppies will run towards a person and try to climb into a lap or jump on legs. A two-way communication system is developing.

During the session, call the puppy to you from 1–1.5 m (3–5 ft) away (on your knees and patting the floor or ground). Walk closely in front of him, and coax him to follow by patting your leg. Sit down on his level for some gentle play. Stroke the puppy. Talk to the puppy; with your voice, try to get him to look at you.

Occasionally, there's a puppy in a litter that acts shy and is uncomfortable when taken to a different room or area. He may not want to come to you or may not even want to walk around and investigate the area by himself. When working with this puppy during his individual session, be sure that you are where the puppy can neither see nor hear his littermates. Sit down on the floor or ground near him. Don't lean over him – that will only make him more fearful. Talk to him in a quiet voice. Pat your hand on the floor in front of him. Try to get his attention. See if you can coax him to come to you even if it's just a matter of his moving a few centimetres. This puppy needs much gentleness. If you're an impatient person, don't try anything that will make you irritated if the puppy doesn't respond the way you think he should. Just spend the time sitting close to the puppy. If neither of you moves for the first session or two, that's the way it is. The puppy will gradually become accustomed to your presence and will begin to approach you and investigate. He should be placed with a person or a family that understands that this puppy will require special attention to develop into a socially functioning puppy, and that he will always remain very sensitive to his environment.

Environmental Enrichment

Beginning with the third week, the puppy is busy learning to use his rapidly developing senses. We know from behavioural and physiological studies how rapidly the puppy's nervous system is growing, and if the senses aren't stimulated, they won't develop into the pathways that give the puppy his best learning potential.

You don't need to dazzle the puppies with a clutter of items. Do your puppies play in the garden? Lawn furniture is an example of environmental stimulation. Moving the wheelbarrow around for clean-up is another example. This is what we mean when we say that a litter raised in a family home environment is automatically socialised and stimulated. However, when puppies are raised in a pen or kennel, specific items need to be added.

Environmental enrichment is as simple as a new surface to walk on (grass) and a new object to investigate (handbag).

Use whatever is available to you. For example, set a couple of old wood stumps in the pen area. Cardboard boxes are marvellous and fall in the easy-come, easy-go category. These can be dens for a puppy to go into or tunnels to walk through. An item that's very popular with one breeder's puppies is a

PHOTO © GAYLE

This rather elaborate play area offers a great deal of enjoyment and enrichment.

wooden box about 1.2 m (4 ft) long and 60 cm (2 ft) wide, open on the ends, with carpet. The puppy can go in one door and out the other or lie inside and look out, or run through, or whatever seems right at the time. Another idea is short lengths of plastic or ceramic pipe – whichever size your puppies can easily walk through. (Never take a chance with a pipe that might become too narrow as the puppies grow.)

Toys

The first concern in selecting toys is safety; obviously, toys should not be breakable or sharp. A wide range of chewing and play toys is available in pet supply shops, but a puppy isn't interested in how much money you spend. For a young puppy, a good toy is something he can pick up in his mouth or push and roll with his nose. A small plastic bottle with a pebble in it for noise is great fun for a puppy. For safe chew toys, a pet supply shop is the best source. (All puppies need chew toys for their human's sake!)

Puppies have preferences, and what attracts one may not interest another. A toy has no value if it's too large, and it's dangerous if it is too small. A sturdy glove is a good toy. A worn-out leather glove is ideal; think of the wealth of odours it has! A couple of knotted socks of different textures can be a lot of fun for puppies who like to shake a toy. Rotate the toys so that a different selection can be available every few days.

Not all puppies are fortunate enough to start their lives with caring and informed breeders. But those who do have an invaluable head start. We appreciate the fact that a large number of breeders in all breeds in all parts of the country look at this labour as one of love.

PHOTO © JUDITH STROM

A favourite toy of one puppy may not interest another. Rotate toys frequently to keep the selection interesting.

CHAPTER 5

Puppy Goes to a New Home

Nothing equals the excitement of anticipating a new puppy! The fun of bringing a puppy home and introducing him to his new family is a very special experience. What hopes we have for our perfect puppy! He will, of course, become a well-mannered dog, staying quietly at our side, eager to follow our every command. Well, it's a long road from the cuddly puppy to the mature dog, but with some effort and understanding, it can be travelled successfully. It all begins with Day One in the new home.

The first few days in a new home can be difficult for both the puppy and the new owner, because both are trying to adjust to a new situation. After all, the puppy finds that he has been suddenly taken from his den and littermates and is expected to immediately accept a new, foreign way of life. With patience and a sense of humour on the part of the new owner, the first few days can be a positive experience for humans and puppy.

*Enjoy getting acquainted
with your dog, but don't expect
too much too soon.*

Preparations

Before the puppy arrives at your home, we assume that you will have made adequate preparations, such as:

- knowing where the puppy will be kept when you're absent from home during the day (garden, kennel or a puppy-proof room)
- knowing where you want the puppy to urinate and defecate
- preparing a bed with a blanket or a piece of carpet in it
- having a supply of puppy food on hand, plus separate food and water bowls
- purchasing a few toys appropriate for the size of your puppy.

You will be much more relaxed if you have thought out these details before the puppy arrives. And the puppy will be more content knowing he has his own area and something to cuddle and chew on as he adjusts.

Age of the Puppy

Many breeders agree that eight to ten weeks is a good age range for a puppy to go to his new home. This puts the puppy in his new environment at the peak of his bonding and socialising period. In families where there are preschoolers, we strongly recommend that a puppy not be introduced into the home during the eighth week.

PHOTO © JUDITH STROM

The seven- to ten-week-old puppy still needs a lot of rest and will take morning and afternoon naps. For the first day or two, however, he might be very excited and spend much of the day in motion, checking out his new home. As long as he isn't hurting himself or anything else in the environment, let him investigate wherever and whatever takes his fancy.

If, for any reason, the puppy is eight weeks old when he first goes to his new home, be very patient with him. This is the fear period, and sharp noises or harsh treatment will leave him with fear that may take months to overcome. Let him take his time

Don't allow children to overtire the puppy.

getting acquainted with everything, and don't take him to places where he will be subjected to loud and frightening sounds or activities. If at all possible, trips to the vet should be arranged either before or after the eighth week.

If the puppy is ten to 12 weeks old when you first bring him home, he'll be more rambunctious, especially if he's one of the larger breeds, and he'll sleep considerably less during the day. However, he's at an age where you can get his attention quite easily and where he'll want to please you and stay close to you. *It's very important that the puppy's pre-training activities begin now.*

The First Day

The main concern with the first few days is letting the puppy get acquainted. Within the area where he is allowed to roam, give him lots of time on his own to sniff and explore, to find his bed area, to determine good nap-taking spots and to learn where his food and water dishes are kept. Feed him a good-quality puppy food; the breeder of the puppy will inform you what the puppy is currently eating. The seven- to eight-week-old puppy is probably eating four times a day, which can be changed to three times a day and, around four to six months of age, to twice a day. We prefer scheduled mealtimes to free feeding because it helps with house-training. In addition, it shows your puppy how reliable you are in the food department — same place, same time, same good food every day. As your puppy grows, you'll gradually need to increase the amount of his food, but don't let him get fat. Sometimes, because of an owner's work schedule, free feeding is the better solution. In this case, the main concern is that the puppy doesn't overeat. Measure the amount of food put in the food dish to keep a record of the quantity being eaten.

> *Ideally, someone should be scheduled to be at home with the new puppy on his first few days. The basis for training habits begins NOW.*

If the puppy is going to be kept in a pen area for a certain amount of time each day, be certain that he has a few toys available, and be certain that he won't be left for long periods of time. The ideal situation is for a puppy to be with someone a good bit of the time for the first week or two. The best time to initiate a puppy into your life, especially if the family is working or at school most of the day, is to arrange for the puppy's arrival during a period when someone will be at home on holiday, at least for the first several days of the puppy's arrival.

The most difficult part of the puppy's first day is the first night in a new and strange place. This subject deserves a section of its own.

First Night Alone

The puppy's first night alone in his new home can be one of intense fear. The fear of suddenly being left alone can lead to anxiety that can show up later as a behavioural problem, such as excessive barking or digging at the carpet.

There aren't many alternatives for a puppy's first night, and it is certain to be a stressful experience to some degree, but there is one method that works very well. Let the puppy spend his first couple of nights in the bedroom of his new master. Put a box in the room with a blanket or carpet in it, or just put the bedding on the floor beside your bed. The puppy might ignore your efforts and select his own place, like under the bed or in a corner. Let the puppy stay wherever he will relax and settle down.

Keeping the puppy in the bedroom the first two nights makes the adjustment to a new home much easier for both puppy and people.

A puppy is usually exhausted by night-time and will sleep through the night. If not, a hand reaching down in the dark helps to calm him. (If this doesn't work, you'd better get up and take the puppy out to urinate.) First thing in the morning, carry the puppy outdoors or to the area covered with newspapers. You usually will have to carry him, because he might not be able to walk as far as that by himself without urinating until he's ten to 12 weeks old.

Two nights, or sometimes three, is usually enough of this special treatment. By then the puppy should be ready to accept his bed in the regular place that you have selected for him. If you don't plan to allow the puppy to continue sleeping in your room, it's best not to let him stay past the third night. If you wait much past that time, the puppy will reach a point where he won't want to be moved and you'll be back to where you started with the crying. If these special measures aren't possible, buy some ear plugs and be prepared for loud crying for at least two nights.

You may want to consider allowing the puppy to continue sleeping in the bedroom. If you work and are away from home a lot, this is one way of giving your dog a sense of your presence and of your desire to be with him as much as possible. If you decide to do this, you should keep the puppy in a crate during the night, or put the puppy on a short rope tied to a leg of the bed until he's house-trained, with his own bedding there also, of course. The rope should be short enough to allow him to lie down without getting tangled.

First Visit to a Vet

Your vet is a vital member of the puppy-raising team. We believe that it makes good sense to select your vet and preferably get acquainted, before you even select the right puppy for yourself. Vets deal with many breeds of dogs in sickness and in health and are only too happy to counsel you during that important time when you are making decisions about dog ownership and familiarising yourself with the do's and don'ts.

Your vet, if consulted early in your puppy's life, will be able to advise you of the things that you should be looking for and will make arrangements in advance for complete health counselling, check-ups and vaccinations.

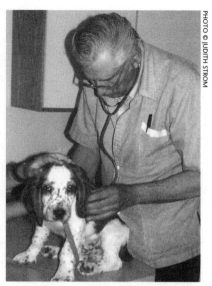

A vet will establish a health care programme for your puppy.

If you have already acquired a puppy and have not yet consulted with a vet, *put this book down and do so right now.* The vet may not want you to come in immediately, but he or she will then make sure that a plan for a healthy and happy future for your puppy is worked out with you and subsequently carried out.

House-Training

Have you ever put a puppy outdoors, left him there for 15 to 20 minutes, and then let him in again only to have him immediately make a puddle or a pile on the carpet? It's very easy to believe that he's doing this on purpose, and it's very easy to get angry. However, the puppy simply doesn't have it all figured out yet. For one reason or another, he's still confused about the indoor–outdoor situation. Besides that, he doesn't urinate and defecate until he has the urge, and he didn't happen to get the urge until he was in on the carpet. It's going to take some time on your part to help him get the whole procedure straightened out. Some puppies learn in a few days, some not until they're three or four months old. Some puppies simply don't have the muscular control until they're several months old.

People tend to get very excited over the process of house-training. What's needed is a realistic philosophy – plus a lot of paper towels and carpet deodorant.

At what age can you expect your puppy to be reliable in the house? The answer is as variable as the puppies to which it applies. In puppy classes, we have owners who say that their puppy had only two accidents and has been trained ever since. Other owners say that their puppy is four months old and sometimes still has an accident. Some puppies adapt to a routine very quickly, and some people adapt to being consistent in training. Some puppies have stronger muscle and bladder control than others. There are many factors that affect the age at which your puppy will be reliably house-trained.

As explained in the discipline section, spanking does more harm than good, and this is especially true in house-training. Many puppies react negatively to spanking. This can create additional problems and often actually prolong the training procedure. The least painful approach for both the owner and the puppy is to establish a routine and to praise the puppy for performance at the proper time in the proper place.

Guidelines for House-Training

- **Feed the puppy at the same times** every day, and when he's finished eating, immediately take him outdoors. Take the puppy out immediately after he awakens from a nap and after a play period, or even in the middle of a play period if it's a long and vigorous one.

- **Keep your puppy in the same room with you** where you can watch him. If necessary, tether him to you by tying a long line around your waist so that the puppy can't get more than 1–1.2 m (3–4 ft) away from you.

- When you can't keep an eye on him in the house, **put him outdoors or keep him in his crate** – not longer than two hours for eight- to ten-week-old puppies, and not longer than three to four hours for older puppies. Every time he comes out of his crate, take him outdoors immediately.

- If you are gone during the day and the puppy is kept in the house, **confine him to a puppy pen or a room that's easy to clean** and that can be mostly covered with newspapers. Gradually decrease the space covered by paper to only one small area. When the puppy is older, probably around three months of age, remove the paper and train him for outdoors only.

- Take the puppy to the **same outdoor area each time**, and stand around and wait. If he doesn't do anything, return to the house, leaving him outdoors for a while if possible. Watch him, then go out and praise him if he does anything. If he comes in without doing his chores, take him back out every five or ten minutes until he has success.

- **Praise, praise, praise** every time your puppy does his chores in an appropriate place. Praise shows the puppy what you want him to do and where.

- If you catch your puppy in the act in the wrong place, **don't spank**, but rush him outdoors.

- **Clean up and deodorise the soiled area** with either a vinegar–water solution (one part vinegar to four parts water) or a commercial cleaner.

Otherwise, when a puppy gets a whiff of that particular odour, an eliminative reflex is set off, and thereafter he does what is natural for him.

- For night-time, **remove the water dish a couple of hours before bedtime**. Take him outdoors at bedtime, then put him either in a small, easily cleaned room or in his crate at your bedside. A puppy can sleep several hours in a crate, and he will awaken you when he needs to go outdoors. Most puppies adjust to their owners' sleep schedule reasonably quickly, depending on the age of the puppy.

- **Use a key phrase**, such as 'hurry up'. This will help in the future to cue your dog to get busy and stop daydreaming.

For the puppy that is still not housebroken by four to four and a half months of age, get busy with your puppy training. Evaluate the relationship between you and your puppy. Does the puppy respond to you when he hears his name? Does he come to you when you call from a short distance? Maybe your puppy thinks that the house is his and that he can do whatever, wherever he wishes.

House-training is your responsibility. The puppy only does what comes naturally. Remember that he is a pack animal and needs to know the rules of the den – the house. Consistent training will be well worth the effort.

Using Crates and Kennels

Another means of controlling the puppy so that he doesn't have accidents when you're not at home is to train him to stay in a crate. As with everything else in puppy training, this is done gradually. Have the crate always available, leaving the door open. Drop pieces of his food inside, and he'll quickly become very happy about going in to eat the pieces. Use it as his bed if possible. You can feed him in it. When you first close the door, stay with him, talking to him in a calm tone. Open the door after a few minutes and praise him, even if he did make a fuss. It will gradually become his 'place' and he'll feel very secure there.

PHOTO © JUDITH STROM

If you leave the crate door open and place a biscuit inside, your puppy will decide this is his special place.

The puppy shouldn't be confined continuously (except at night), but a crate can be a big help for an hour or two at a time. As the puppy grows older, he can spend longer periods of time in a crate as long as it isn't a regular long-term arrangement. A crate is also excellent for car travel. It keeps the dog safe from sudden stops and swerves, and it keeps the people safe from an excitable dog.

> *Crates can be a good training tool, and are only cruel if misused.*

There's nothing cruel about using a crate. It's very natural for a dog, because it fits into his den concept. Most dogs that have their own crates consider them a place of security. The only conceivable problems arise if the puppy is forced into the cage suddenly and becomes frightened, or if he is left in it for hours at a time and becomes excessively lonely and bored.

Some families find a garden kennel or pen area a necessity for confining the dog to a particular area of the garden. This offers protection for flowers and landscaping during the puppy's rambunctious growing-up months or when the puppy is left outdoors with no people present. Pens can be made of chain link and can be an attractive area, easy to keep clean.

Care must be taken, however, not to put the puppy in his kennel and then forget about him. Everyone these days is busy, but if you're too busy to have the puppy out of the kennel every day to be with you in the house or in the garden, then you're too busy to have a dog. Garden kennels are a convenience if used properly, but should never be considered for 24-hour-a-day confinement.

The Importance of Play

Play is an important part of the maturation process. A puppy learns what his abilities are by playing – play sharpens the senses of sight and scent. Play also stimulates the brain, keeping the puppy alert and interested in his environment.

Play can be as simple as a running game – inviting the puppy by giving the canine signal for play (a play-bow, putting your hands on your knees and bending over). Take a quick step, and the puppy will probably start running around you in a circle. After the puppy learns his name, you can play hide-and-seek – hide when you call him to come to you. Run up the stairs or to the next room, or behind a door. Keep calling until he finds you and discovers how happy you are to see him. Another running game is the round-robin. Position family members or friends around the garden. Take turns calling the puppy, and have each person praise the puppy enthusiastically for coming before the next person calls him.

A variety of toys encourages play, and a toy box on the floor for storage keeps them from cluttering the house. A squeaky toy and a puppy is a delightful combination, with the puppy pouncing, tossing, talking and seeing how much noise he can produce. Soft stuffed toys made for dogs are marvellous fun, but if your puppy will rip it apart, it can't be left in the toy box; just get it out for short periods of time when you can watch. Put a knotted sock in the toy box for this puppy. One puppy had a teddy bear for his favourite toy, and he never

This puppy has a clean, secure pen with clean water and plenty of toys for those times when he must be left unattended.

chewed it – he just carried it around – and it was still a favourite two years later. This, however, is an exception.

Balls are great toys. To begin, just sit on the floor with your legs out and roll the ball. When your puppy has it, pat the floor to encourage the puppy to run back to you. With an older puppy, bounce the ball and let the puppy learn to catch it in the air. Balls designed to roll in crazy directions are a delight for many puppies. Retrieving is a good game for exercising your puppy.

Chew toys serve multiple purposes – puppies love something hard to vent their chewing desire, and this also starts to wear off the sharpest points of their baby teeth. Sterilised bones, Nylabones and rawhide pieces serve this purpose. Use rawhide sparingly if your puppy tears it apart too quickly and swallows the pieces. Shoes, socks, magazines, handbags, tennis balls and old leather gloves are also some of a puppy's more favourite toys. If you don't want your puppy chewing these items, keep them out of reach.

Play hide-and-seek with your puppy's toys. Put a toy behind a piece of furniture. 'Where's the squeaky? Find it!' Help him to find it until he learns the game. Use the name of his favourite toys often. Pretty soon, he'll learn which toy to go and get from his toy box when you call it by name.

Tug toys are a very popular item in pet shops and can be used either to good advantage or, with some puppies, should not be used at all. For independent puppies that don't have much interest in playing with you, a tug-of-war game allows you and your puppy to interact with each other and to develop your own version of the game. For other puppies, tug-of-war games encourage aggressiveness or excessive mouthiness. These puppies obviously shouldn't play this type of game. A rule of thumb to determine how much of this characteristic is in your puppy is to note his tendency to get too excited and your inability to halt the game. If the puppy won't stop, tears your shirt sleeve, grabs at your hand and loses control of his bite inhibition, this game isn't for him.

Most puppies will readily play with other dogs and puppies, as well as by themselves with a favourite toy, but the play that we truly want to encourage is a one-on-one activity. It's worth the effort, because there's nothing sadder than a grown dog that doesn't know how to have fun with his people.

Puppies and Older Dogs

Young puppies should never be left alone with older dogs unless you know beyond a doubt how the older dog treats rambunctious youngsters. There's a good reason for this. Some puppies don't begin to show submissiveness until they're about four months of age. Until they reach that point, they don't have an ounce of sense around older dogs and will usually pester them until the mature dog puts a stop to it. This might be done in a manner that doesn't injure a dog, such as scruff-shaking or snapping and growling. However, it might also be done with a bite that could injure a small puppy seriously. Don't ever take that chance.

By the time the puppy is four months old, the risk of injury becomes much less. The puppy begins to assume the submissive posture of rolling on his side when threatened by an older dog, and this acts as a damper on the situation. A puppy at least four months old knows enough to move out of the way quickly, too.

PHOTO © JUDITH STROM

Never leave a new puppy alone with an older dog. Take special care when introducing the puppy until you are absolutely sure he will be safe.

CHAPTER 6

Socialisation Continues

With the information gathered from brain research in recent years, we are beginning to understand the whys of working with our puppies at an early age. 'The more sensory stimulation that the dog's brain receives', states Bruce Fogle, DVM, in *The Dog's Mind*, 'the more developed his mind will become'. Sensory and physical activities cause nerve cells (neurons) in the brain to grow and make new synaptic connections with other nerve cells. This results in a network that expands to accommodate and assimilate new information.

Prepare Your Eight- to 16-week-old Puppy for the Future

Experiences during the puppy's first months determine the actual wiring of the brain. Each time your puppy learns a new activity, makes eye contact, responds to your voice or plays with you and others (including dogs), he stimulates the connections in the networks of the brain. These connections, called synapses, are strengthened when stimulated and become part of the brain's permanent structures. If the synapses receive no signals from the neurons, they wither away.

The growth of the dog's brain is complete in half a year compared to 18 years in humans. Think about that. And about how fast these first puppy weeks fly by.

How do you deal with those neuron responsibilities? Take a leave of absence from your job? Spend at least 12 hours a day with your puppy? Smother him with structured activities? No, that's not necessary. But plan to give your puppy as large a variety of experiences as you can during these early months. If you work, your puppy should be top priority when you're home.

Stimulate those Neurons

Physical activities introduce a variety of challenges that stimulate the growth of brain cells. Help your puppy navigate the rungs of a ladder lying on the ground and walk a board about 60 cm (2 ft) wide, 60 cm (2 ft) off the ground. Teach him to climb an A-frame (or any inclined surface that has cleats), run through a tunnel (available in toy shops or you can use a long box with ends removed) and climb up and down wide stairs. Other activities include jumping over fallen branches or a broomstick set 15–20 cm (6–8 in) off the ground. Don't try to show off and have your puppy jump higher. The same goes for taking your puppy jogging with you. At this age, the puppy should have short walks. The joints shouldn't be stressed. Check with your vet.

If puppy classes in your town are outdoors and, because of the vaccination schedule, you want to wait until your puppy is four months of age, you can devise these and similar exercises at home. Use your imagination. You don't need specially constructed items. Introduce these activities at as young an age as possible.

PHOTO © CLARICE RUTHERFORD

New experiences for your puppy can be found around the house.

Mental exercises stimulate the growth of brain cells and the connecting synapses. Teach your puppy to catch a treat. Practice makes perfect. Later, add catching a bouncing ball. Teach him the names of his toys by repeating the name when you play with him. One day he'll surprise you by bringing the toy you ask for. Hide a dog biscuit in the room for your puppy to find by sniffing. Let him watch you, then help by guiding him close to it. After he knows the game, teach him to find a favourite toy.

If you repeat the name of the toy you play with, one day your puppy will select the one you ask for.

The best part about having fun with your puppy is that he uses his senses – looking, listening, scenting, touching and tasting (a variety of titbits keeps his interest high). His agility increases with all of the different movements and with the muscle and mental activity required.

Teach Eye Contact

You want your puppy to look at you when he hears his name. (Don't overdo this. A hundred times a day is *not* good.) At ten to 12 weeks, the puppy wants to look at you because you are his world. Take advantage of this. Each time he responds to his name and makes eye contact, reward him with 'good dog' or a command

Praise your puppy lavishly each time he responds to his name and makes eye contact with you.

such as 'come' or 'sit' when he knows them. Sometimes, as a reward, clap your hands or scratch behind his ears – *do anything that's fun.*

PHOTO © JUDITH STROM

Agility obstacles provide excellent stimulation for the puppy.

Some puppies, especially independent, shy and very active puppies, need your feedback even if they only begin to turn the head in your direction. The more hesitant, distracted or busy your puppy is, the more you need to work on the timing of your praise the instant he looks towards you. Teach your family about this. Children are notorious for nagging a dog by repeating his name. Then, when the puppy does look, the kids are distracted, forget what they were doing and ignore the dog. Adults have this problem, too. A friend complained that her four-month-old puppy never paid any attention to her. While we visited the park, I watched her call his name three times within 20 seconds. He glanced at her twice, but she never said 'good' or smiled or in any way acknowledged his glance. The third time, of course, he didn't bother looking. You should expect your puppy to pay attention to you. But first you must concentrate on what you are doing and pay attention to your puppy.

If you have other dogs living at home, make the effort to spend time with the puppy one-on-one. Take your puppy with you whenever you can to buy dog food at a pet shop or to visit a friend. Take him for walks. If you know of a field or area that has ups and downs, rocks, fallen trees and branches, that's ideal. And, of course, use some of your time together just having fun.

Socialise Your Puppy

It's easy for us to get preachy about this because it's so **vitally important**. It's difficult for you, the puppy owner, to know what the fuss is all about because you don't see any specific results from your socialisation activities. And you probably can't recognise the behaviours at one to two years of age that are symptoms of a lack of socialisation or indicators of success, because you will naturally assume that your dog's behaviour has nothing to do with his activities when he was two to four months of age (and seven to nine months of age, which is a secondary socialisation period).

Here are the facts. The under-socialised dog often becomes fearful of anything new – people, dogs, places, anything. This is shown by excessive barking, anxiety, dog aggression, fear and hyperactivity. The socialised dog is confident around people and other dogs and seldom displays anxiety in new environments. Best of all, he will calm down after a vigorous play period rather than stay wound up. Socialisation introduces more learning experiences. The under-socialised dog has a brain that lacks the huge array of neural connections of the well-socialised dog that lives in an enriched environment with toys and home activities.

How do you socialise your puppy? Quite easily. If it's available for you where you live, a puppy kindergarten class brings together new puppies and new people in a new environment. You get a lot for your tuition fee. Choose places that are safe to take your puppy, because you probably haven't finished your puppy-shot series yet. This includes visiting neighbours, friends and outdoor areas that you know aren't frequented by dogs running at large. Some pet supply shops are happy if dogs accompany their customers.

Think about the potential places and people in your town and about your lifestyle. There might be more possibilities for socialisation than you realise. If you're gone during the day, leave the radio or TV on and have toys that can be stuffed with biscuits or cheese. Change toys daily. A rawhide chewy might ease the stress of departure time for both of you.

Socialising your puppy isn't complicated, nor does it involve anything that is not a part of your life or your family's life. But please remember – *there is so much to do, and such a short time in which to do it.*

Take your puppy with you whenever you can.

PHOTO © KENT DANNEN

Introduce the Puppy to Pre-training Activities

Building self-confidence and teaching a puppy to do different things is a round-robin situation. The more confidence a puppy has, the better he learns. By the same token, when a puppy is learning to do new things, he is also gaining more confidence in himself and in his abilities.

This type of puppy activity is not a rigid training session. We're working with emotionally immature animals that are susceptible to fears and to confidence-destroying tactics similar to those that affect the human child. The term 'pre-training' better indicates the intent of these activities, assuming that such a term does not belittle their importance. We assure you, work at this age will pay big dividends in the learning attitude of your dog when he is older.

The Collar

Puppies should become comfortable wearing a buckle collar at eight weeks of age. Continually check the collar for tightness, because puppies often grow in spurts and a collar can become too tight in a very short time. Do not use chain or slip collars with puppies. It is a legal requirement for a dog to wear a collar and tag bearing the owner's name and address when the dog is out in a public place.

The Leash

Puppies need to learn about leashes, which should be as lightweight as possible. Thick leashes, whether they are made of leather or cotton webbing, are too stiff and heavy. A lightweight leash will be usable long after your puppy grows up. Chain leashes aren't acceptable.

Leash Training

Clip the leash to the collar, and when the puppy starts walking, go his way. Follow for a minute or two, then release the puppy from the leash. Another suggestion: Some puppies get very excitable on the leash, so when the puppy is in the garden and ready to go back into the house, put the leash on him when he's trotting happily. He'll be intent on returning to his home area and shouldn't be bothered by the leash. Then there's the puppy that insists on chewing the leash. Encourage him to pay attention to you by coaxing with your voice and patting your leg as you walk. Keep the puppy moving at a brisk pace – almost a run – to keep his attention on you. If he insists on tugging the leash, spray some Bitter Apple, available at pet supply shops, on the part the puppy usually grabs.

The Sit

Hold a titbit right on top of the puppy's nose, and move it back parallel to the floor. The puppy will sit as his head moves back to follow the titbit. Praise him as soon as he sits. Some puppies need numerous repetitions over several days before they will sit. Give praise and a treat every time the puppy bends his back legs. He will soon sit.

Good hand position for teaching the sit. The leash is used for training in the park but isn't needed in the house.

Begin teaching the come as close as necessary to get the puppy's attention.

The Come

Teach the come anytime and any place around the house or garden. You do not need to have a leash on your puppy for this. The young puppy loves to come running and lick you in the face. Remember, you are his whole world. Take advantage of this, especially with the shy or the independent puppy that might initially resist coming to you. Get the puppy excited while you are standing right in front of him, then run backwards several metres. Give lots of happy praise and a titbit – even independent puppies usually can't resist a little piece of sausage or cheese. If your puppy is busy and easily distracted, begin the come

Introduce the puppy to grooming in a comfortable place.

at very short distances – maybe 1–1.2 m (3–4 ft). Begin as close as necessary to get the puppy's attention and to achieve success. Gradually lengthen the distance. What's important at this stage is the puppy's attitude – he wants to come running to you *because it's such fun*.

Grooming

Brushing should be included in the puppy's routine by this time. Begin very gradually. Thirty seconds is long enough to have the puppy standing (relatively still) while you brush him. Praise him when you are able to accomplish a couple of brushes. This is important, because the puppy must know when he has pleased you. Gradually increase the length of time you work with the puppy. You'll notice a slow, steady improvement in his co-operation. If you've timed your praise well, the puppy will realise that grooming is a pleasant experience to be shared with you even though tangles might occasionally complicate the situation. While you work with your puppy, tell him how handsome he is and how well he's behaving. Handle the puppy's feet every time you groom, and clip nails every week or two.

If you're wishy-washy in your attitude towards grooming and towards having the puppy stand still for a minute, your puppy will sense this. He will take advantage of you and will never stand still. In this case, read the next chapter on moulding the behaviour of your puppy.

Sometimes a puppy needs a confidence boost.

Important Basics when Teaching Puppies

Here are some basic guidelines that you can adopt as you work with your puppy to teach him good house manners.

- **Don't Get Tough**
  Emotionally and psychologically, the puppy is extremely sensitive. This means that learning takes place quickly, but that fears can also occur easily and thus inhibit learning. Puppies cannot take pressure or harsh treatment. Repetition is the key.

- **Keep It Simple**
  A puppy learns to do things in a step-by-step manner. If you expect a puppy to do something before you've properly taught him to do it, he will lose his confidence and will learn not to try. The same puppy, given a simple, step-by-step training approach, will become a dog that is eager to learn and ready for more complicated training as he gets older.

- **Be Brief**
  Puppies have a very short attention span. A puppy learns only while he pays attention to you, and you won't accomplish anything if you keep on

PHOTO ROSEMARY SHELTON © CLICK THE PHOTO CONNECTION

This puppy is learning basic agility skills at a kindergarden class.

training when the puppy is mentally tired, even though physically he may still be very lively.

• **Build Confidence**

Relax while you're with the puppy. Smile at him, speak in a pleasant voice, and play running games with him. It's important at this age for the puppy to feel that he's a valuable individual. Do your training exercises in a relatively quiet place around the house and garden. Because he's so playful, the puppy is easily distracted by other people and activities. If he's constantly being interrupted by other sights and sounds, it will be difficult for him to get the message that you enjoy being with him and that you think he's wonderful.

• **Use Words**

Don't expect your puppy to be a mind reader. The only way that he'll learn to associate the command with the action is if you use the word every time you guide him into doing what you want. A puppy can learn a large vocabulary with words such as 'outdoors', 'bedtime', and 'go for a walk', as well as the common commands.

• **Don't Expect Overnight Results**

Try to stay relaxed as you work with the puppy. Puppies learn in spurts and starts. One day, he may know absolutely everything and perform to perfection. The next day, it's as though he never had a moment's training. Too many owners make the mistake of thinking that if their puppy does it right once or twice, he knows it forever. But it really takes hundreds of repetitions for a puppy to learn something. He may go through several periods of confusion in the process. You may think that he's mad at you or is trying to spite you. In reality, he's probably trying to tell you that he's confused for some reason. This is often caused by some unknown factor. Perhaps you've done something a little differently, or the environment has changed in some way and his confidence has been shaken. Continue with your training programme. It will all iron out with time and effort.

If you take these suggestions into consideration, you are automatically teaching your puppy to pay attention. By adhering to his physical and psychological needs, you'll find that he will respond to you and you will be well on your way to building a good puppy–person relationship.

CHAPTER 7

Domesticating Your Puppy

Much of a puppy's future behaviour is set by what he experiences between three and 16 weeks of age. His basic attitude towards people and his desire to please are established during these weeks. This chapter discusses the many ways in which new owners can mould the behaviour of the puppy aged eight weeks and upwards to fit into their lifestyle. This is the age when the owner and the puppy's environment both exert a very strong influence in the development of the puppy's maturing personality. *Hard work during this period pays big dividends for the rest of the dog's life.*

Shaping Behaviour

It may come as a surprise to learn that your puppy is already developing behaviour habits from the day he enters his new home. You can use this to your advantage immediately. For instance, a puppy can learn to sit for his food dish before he even knows the sit command.

Hold the food dish up, back and over the puppy's head. The instant his rear moves in a sitting direction, get the dish to the floor. The first few times you try this, the puppy may not look as if he's going to sit. Try to time the food dish delivery with a bending of the puppy's hind legs. After several days of good timing on your part, the puppy will sit when he sees you with the food dish. This

> *Barring extremes of shyness or aggressiveness, there is enough potential variation of behavioural patterns that you'll be able to modify your puppy's behaviour to fit in with your lifestyle. You do this by encouraging the characteristics that you like.*

is an example of how easily a puppy's behaviour can be moulded, beginning as early as seven weeks of age.

A puppy can just as easily be conditioned to bite your trouser leg or to bark at you. If your response is to pick him up and hold him in an effort to stop the behaviour, the puppy perceives this as a reward (even though unintentional on your part) and therefore sees the behaviour as acceptable.

A puppy's behaviour is moulded all day long in this same manner. Whenever we praise the puppy, or pat or cuddle him, the behaviour immediately preceding the attention is being encouraged. Whenever we speak sharply or distract the puppy or discipline him, the behaviour is being discouraged. Puppies develop habits very quickly. If you can control your behaviour and pay attention to what actions you're rewarding, you're going to end up with a nice dog that you'll be happy to have around the house. It's much easier to encourage good behaviour than to change bad behaviour after the puppy has been allowed to get away with it.

Always encourage good behaviour.

The Bonding Process

Bonding occurs most readily between the age of seven to 16 weeks. To ensure that a puppy will be responsive to his owner as well as to other people throughout the rest of his life, he needs to bond to someone at this age. From a puppy's perspective, bonding means that he has someone to respect, to trust, to play with and to show him what he can and cannot do. He has someone who cares. To you, bonding means that your puppy will follow you around the house and look to you for approval of his just being there.

Bonding is the process of putting yourself first in your puppy's priorities. It's your puppy looking at you when you say his name; it's your puppy coming to you when you call him, rather than running on past. To accomplish this bonding takes time spent one-on-one with your puppy, taking walks with your puppy and not giving up if your puppy doesn't respond as readily as you think he should. The independent, dominant or overly busy puppy can reach a high degree of bonding if you keep working with him. So don't throw your hands up in impatience.

An excellent way to begin the bonding process is to tether your puppy to you (assuming he is already leash-trained.) Put your puppy on a 2 m (6 ft) leash and tie it around your waist or through a belt loop. The leash must be long enough for the puppy to be able to sit or lie down, but you don't want a cord so long that it lets him wander some distance away from you. As you go about your business around the house, don't give your puppy any commands such as sit or down. If he insists on jumping, give a quick, downward tug on the leash close to the collar. Prohibit biting or chewing by a swift bump or a sharp 'no!' Tether your puppy for at least 20 minutes (longer if possible) for several days. Your puppy is beginning his one-on-one relationship with you. The more independent your puppy's personality, the more he needs this process.

Tethering can be done anywhere around the house.

A major aspect of the bonding process involves establishing yourself as the alpha member of your puppy's new pack. Your role as pack leader begins when you bring the puppy home, and it is a matter, at this age, of your attitude and approach to discipline. You need to give special attention to how you teach your puppy about good house manners, and you need to learn what disciplines you should and shouldn't use.

Discipline

Very few of us live with the perfect puppy. A busy puppy, full of joyful energy, can get himself in trouble because he doesn't know what he can and can't do around the house. We use discipline to correct a puppy's bad (from our point of view) behaviour. When we correct a behaviour, we are saying to the puppy, 'I want your attention right now. What you're doing is not okay'. We want to halt that behaviour, gain his full attention, then show him what behaviour we do want from him. Fortunately, a variety of disciplines exist to effectively help the puppy understand what behaviours we don't like. **Praising our puppy's good behaviour helps him to understand what behaviours we do like.**

Punishment

There's no place for punishment with young puppies. Hitting a puppy with a newspaper or spanking with your hand is cruel punishment for any misbehaviour. It certainly appears to be effective because your puppy immediately stops his bad behaviour and looks sorry for what he's done (unless he's dominant-aggressive, in which case he might challenge you), but puppies don't understand this punishment. It works against their natural attraction to people. It can build a wall of defence mechanisms that results in a dog that is more difficult to train and to communicate with when he's older. What you've gained in immediate release of your anger, you've lost in your dog's confidence and total trust.

Another abusive discipline is loud, angry, emotional shouting. A human voice with a nasty tone to it can put a touch of panic in your puppy's mind, or if he's independent, stubborn or dominant, it can make him turn more into himself, becoming more and more unresponsive to you. Your puppy is a baby. The purpose of this book is to help you get your baby dog off to a good start. Puppies do need discipline at times, but it must be the right kind of discipline.

Distraction

Distraction followed by praise works very well in moulding your puppy's behaviour. Much of the mischief that a puppy gets into is a result of busyness. Many behaviours, like pulling on curtains or unrolling a roll of toilet paper by running through the house carrying the end of it, are not repeated once the puppy has been distracted and gone on to other things.

If your puppy is young – seven to 10 weeks old – or is especially sound sensitive, use your voice to distract him. A loud 'uh-uh', a hand clap or a slap on a table to startle the puppy will divert his attention to you. If the puppy is ignoring you, use a shake can. For puppies, a flat-sided pill bottle with a few pennies in it makes an impressive sound to divert a puppy's attention from his

PHOTO © BETH BAILEY

Distract the puppy with a toy and take away what he is chewing.

current mischief. The bottle will fit nicely into your pocket, making it handy and ready for action. When your puppy is involved in a 'no-no', shake the can. The startle effect should stop his action. When he looks up in surprise, distract him, talk to him or call him to you (if you are very close). Then you can praise him for being a good puppy.

Good behaviour consists of simply not doing what he has been doing. If he's not doing whatever it was you didn't like, then he must be a good puppy – so tell him. How else will he know? Your praise is calm, not exciting. You are simply telling him that you prefer his good behaviour over his bad behaviour.

Canine-type Discipline

To teach a puppy that he can't do 'that' anymore, you have to catch him in the act and discipline him. How do adult dogs discipline young dogs? Primarily by using the element of surprise. When the puppy is disciplined for the first time – such as for trying to share a bone – the adult dog might snarl and grab for the puppy. Following that initial discipline, it takes only a curl of the lip or a quiet growl to remind the puppy of what not to touch or where not to go. Of course, with some puppies, particularly the very lively ones, the discipline wears off rather quickly, and then the puppy asks for it again. He is startled into submission, and the cycle of good behaviour begins once again.

Canine disciplines can be effective for you. These are a natural follow-through from consequences that the puppy might have experienced in the litter. When a puppy is playing too roughly with his teeth, the puppy that is being

PHOTO © KENT DANNEN

Puppies first learn discipline from their mother.

chewed on gives a screech and moves away. He won't play anymore. We can imitate this behaviour.

Isolation

PHOTO © CLARICE RUTHERFORD

If your puppy plays too rough, isolate him by totally ignoring him until he calms down.

Isolation is effective because it's an immediate reaction the instant the puppy misbehaves. A puppy is a very social creature, and you are his adult pack member. If you totally withdraw all attention, he's going to be a very unhappy puppy. So – when he's very mouthy and grabs at you when you pet him – say 'off' or 'no bite', and immediately turn your back to him. Fold your arms tightly, and even close your eyes. Do not talk. If he starts to jump on you or if he starts to bark, totally ignore him. Walk away and leave the room if necessary. The puppy should feel completely isolated from you. After about a minute, unfreeze and say 'hi' to your puppy. Tell him that he's a good puppy at that moment and that you hope he will continue to be good. Pat him again, and if he starts mouthing or chewing on you, repeat the isolation. And, of course, repeat the resultant quiet praise. It may take several repetitions in succession, but he should soon get the message.

Time Out

The other method is called 'time out'. When your puppy is doing something that you don't like – such as grabbing and chewing your trouser leg – leave the room for a minute or two, or pick up the puppy and take him to a time-out room (such as the bathroom or the kitchen). Do not shout or use an angry voice. In a minute or two, let him back in, telling him quietly that now he's a good puppy. For extra-lively puppies, divert their attention from the unwanted activity with a toy when they come back in. When you use a time out, don't just go off and leave him there, because then it won't be a learning situation for the puppy. Bring the puppy back in and repeat the time out if necessary. Some puppies need two or three repetitions in a row before they get the message.

Squirt Bottle

Many owners have success using squirt bottles for discipline. It interrupts the puppy in the midst of barking or jumping up or grabbing at hands, and at the same time, the puppy hears the 'quiet' or 'off' command, followed by praise

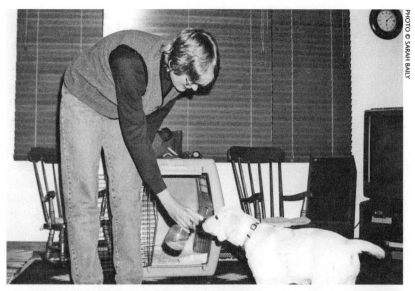

The squirt bottle should be held close to the puppy's mouth. Use a stream, not a spray. If two or three separate uses of the squirt bottle have no efffect on the behaviour, stop using it.

when he is no longer performing the unwanted behaviour. Water bottles work well for a few times, but then puppies tend to treat the water squirt as a game. A most effective spray is a vinegar solution (one part vinegar to either six or four parts water). We have found white vinegar to be effective, but other kinds should work, too. Vinegar seems to be universally distasteful and therefore a successful inhibitor of certain behaviours for puppies from about three months old on through adulthood. Use the stream, not the spray setting, to spray the puppy's mouth, lips and muzzle. A squeeze lemon has the same effect on many puppies, but other puppies seem to like the taste. Still, it's worth a try.

The Sit Command

This command is an important part of the disciplinary process. You give a 'no' command to stop the behaviour, followed immediately with 'sit' to get the puppy to respond to you. This is effective because you not only stop the bad behaviour, you also give the puppy an alternative behaviour for which he can then be praised. Obviously, the puppy needs to know the sit command well enough to be able to respond to it under varying circumstances.

The No Command

Don't overuse this or your puppy will tune it out and it will lose its effectiveness. Decide what bugs you the most and use 'no' to correct these two or three behaviours. For other, less offensive behaviours, use 'uh-uh' or 'wrong'. Once your puppy understands that 'no' means to stop what he's doing, you can begin using it more often, in a speaking tone of voice, and he should stop or at least pause at whatever he is doing.

Let your puppy know when he's being good.

Evaluating the Different Disciplines

Domesticating a puppy involves continual interaction between two individual living beings – the puppy and his owner. We must acknowledge the fact that problems can originate principally with the owner, just as much as with the puppy. In analysing the effect of your teaching methods (discipline is teaching) with your puppy, ask yourself: Is this particular method effective? If not, is any method working? If not, then what is wrong?

At this point, take an objective look at your personality and at your puppy's personality. Is your puppy growing up differently from the way you had anticipated? Do you sometimes think that you're a mismatch? Puppies go through many phases before they mature. Often, if you are patient and keep on doing what you're doing, the puppy will grow out of a particularly difficult stage of behaviour. Encourage and praise the behaviours that make you happy. Distract or discourage the behaviours that you don't like. This is the way you mould your puppy's personality.

While you are evaluating, you must also be aware that there may be an underlying physical or functional abnormality causing the puppy's difficult or seemingly intractable behaviour. Have your puppy checked out by a vet.

Puppies Will Be Puppies

There's a possibility that you may inadvertently exaggerate the degree of the behaviour problem of your puppy. Especially if this is your first puppy, you may not realise that some digging, some chewing, some barking and some jumping up are natural. This is why we keep stressing that it's up to you, the owner, to teach the puppy what to do and what not to do. Puppies are canines, and there are certain behaviours that are simply not wrong from the puppy's point of view. So don't get angry at the puppy just because you decide that he should act more like a person than a dog. Simply get busy and show him what you do and don't want him to do.

Moulding your puppy's behaviour isn't done in a day or two. It takes weeks of praising good behaviour and discouraging bad behaviour. It's a style of living – a daily programme. Repeating the lesson in as many new places as you can will help you and your puppy learn to live together. Lessons learnt at home will need to be repeated elsewhere so that the puppy learns what behaviour you want and not just that the rules apply in your own house.

Accept your puppy as he is, not as you think he should be. If your puppy is shy, it won't help for you to get stern and impatient. Accept the shyness and do what needs to be done. This also applies to the independent puppy and the assertive puppy. Over a period of weeks, you will find that confidence and communication between the two of you are increasing and that your puppy's general behaviour is changing, to your mutual satisfaction.

CHAPTER 8

Development from Three to Six Months

The rapid changes noticeable in the puppy's behaviour during the first three months have levelled off. The central nervous system is now well developed. By three months of age, the puppy's problem-solving ability is functioning well, but his immaturity gets in the way. In other words, he has a short attention span and is too rambunctious to settle down and learn complicated behaviour. However, he's ready to learn simple commands.

This is a delightful age and passes much too quickly. By the end of this period, the large-breed puppies have grown to approximately two-thirds of their mature size, and small breeds may be close to their final height. After six months of age, the puppy will become much more independent, will reach sexual maturity and will be very responsive to physiological stimuli. However, the age from three to six months is still one of puppy charm and innocence. The puppy and people are adjusting to each other, and the puppy is learning what the pack rules are. He's readily able to cope with life by now, he's a willing worker, and he is happy to try whatever you ask (at least most of the time).

This is an age to enjoy – but watch out!
Your puppy is
NOT too good to be true.

Taking the puppy to different places continues to be important at this age. The puppy's environmental awareness is at a peak now. He's ready for anything. Exposure to a variety of places will continue to be a factor in building self-confidence in the puppy and will help him take stressful events in the future in his stride.

The second set of teeth begins to appear during this period, which can cause chewing and biting problems. The puppy needs some items of his own for chewing.

A dog displays dominance by leaning over another dog.

Dominance and Submission

By four months of age, the puppy is beginning to show signs of dominance and submissiveness towards other dogs. Previously, we noted that a young puppy shouldn't be left with irritable older dogs because the puppy wouldn't recognise the dominance signs of the older dog and wouldn't respond with a sign of submission. As a consequence, the puppy might get bitten. However, around four months of age this changes, and the puppy becomes aware that dominance is displayed by direct eye contact, by a tail held straight up and by the dominant dog's putting his head over the puppy's shoulder.

The submissive signs that the puppy will display towards a dominant dog are a flattening of the ears, tucking the tail between the legs and cowering, if not rolling over on the side or back. Usually a puppy is submissive to an older dog, although in some instances a very assertive puppy will soon realise that he can be dominant to an especially submissive adult. With young dogs close in age, some puppies will be dominant over others, and generally a dominant–submissive relationship is established very quickly. With some puppies, it's a change-about situation as they take turns at dominance and submission.

Total submissiveness, lying on the back and exposing the belly, may be demonstrated to another dog or to a person.

The Avoidance Period

Around four months of age, the puppy will go through an avoidance period similar to the fear period experienced at eight weeks. The puppy becomes very hesitant about doing anything new and different. He becomes quite suspicious of anything new that is brought into his home environment and nervous of any new place that he might be visiting.

If your puppy has a quiet personality, he may not respond as happily during training sessions, or he may seem hesitant and a little fearful if you take him to a new place. If this is the case, ease off the training routine. Make it fun; just enjoy being with your puppy.

During the avoidance period, your puppy may not respond as happily during training sessions. It's time to ease off and just have fun with your puppy for a while.

On the other hand, if you have a very independent or assertive puppy, this age may find him in a relatively receptive frame of mind. His being a little apprehensive of new things in his life will tend to make him look to you for support. While he's paying attention to you, get busy and teach him something.

Teething

In many breeds, the puppy teeth are sometimes retained during the period that permanent teeth are erupting. This can have a long-lasting effect. If the puppy teeth are retained, the permanent teeth are forced into an abnormal position. This can lead to permanent problems with the way in which the bite comes together in front. Another problem associated with retention of puppy teeth is damage to the surrounding gum, which can progress to chronic oral disease in adult life.

Bear in mind that the puppy between four and five months is extra-sensitive about his mouth. You should pay careful attention to the possibility of teething problems. If you have any concern that teething is not going well, consult your vet immediately. Puppy teeth may need to be pulled to allow room for the permanent teeth, especially the large canine teeth.

Walking with your puppy helps to put you in the role of leader. Call him to you periodically to enforce your leadership and reward him with a treat for coming to you.

The Leadership Concept

During the three- to six-month age period, the most important help you can give your puppy is to let him know that you're the leader. The puppy as a new member of the family transfers his dependency from his mother to you. **If the balance of this relationship is to be sustained, you must maintain the dominant role in your puppy's life.**

The dog is not a democratic animal. If you allow your puppy equal say in his activities, he will interpret that as permission to do whatever he wants. He will begin to guide your activities to coincide with his benefits. He'll determine such things as where he wants to sleep, how often he wants to be let in and out of the house and how much attention he gets. A dog with a more aggressive personality may even go to the extent of not letting you touch his food or

> *Even the most well-behaved puppies need to be reminded you are the leader of the pack.*

growling or snapping if you try to make him do something that he doesn't want to do.

An extremely important and necessary factor in raising a puppy is to establish your dominance. This involves a conscious effort on your part. It's very easy to let these three months slide by and to think that your puppy doesn't need training because he's such a good dog. But in a few months, you'll regret that decision. The sweet puppy that never needed puppy training because he never did anything wrong begins to exercise his mature personality. He's not mean, but suddenly he's a lively handful that isn't paying attention to you because the pattern of communication wasn't established as a puppy. This applies to the toy breeds as well as to the large breeds. Three to six months is a good age to reinforce your dominant role. Because the puppy still wants to be close to you, it's easy to get his attention and also easy to discipline him.

The Pack Structure

As discussed earlier, even though the dog has not lived the life of his ancestor, the wolf, for tens of thousands of years, he still retains some of the instincts. One of these is the pack structure. The wolf cannot survive without a pack structure – and neither can the dog, at least not happily. If a wolf is put out of the pack, he lives on the fringe for a while. He goes searching for another single wolf who will join him. If this doesn't happen, he probably won't survive. It takes at least two wolves to kill a large animal. A diet of many small rodents isn't enough for an active wolf.

In the wolf pack, the leader is alpha. The beta wolf is second-in-command.

The domesticated dog lives in a people pack – the family. The leader is alpha, the one the dog will obey. Two adults can work together, both of them receiving the alpha respect of their dog. He needs to be with his pack, playing and working

PHOTO © JUDITH STROM

Maintain your leadership by asking your puppy to obey simple commands like come.

together. This is a strong instinct. The most miserable thing that can happen to a dog is to be left alone in the garden or pen because no one has time for him.

Understanding the pack instinct and how it affects your puppy's behaviour can help you to relate to and train your puppy in a way that will keep both you and him happy.

The Family Pack

Anyone who has been involved in maintaining a small group of dogs together in a common environment will know that they establish a social order that has a leader. Because your dog is a dog, he is very aware of social order and will find his position sooner or later in the family situation. Many people assume that they are the dominant leader on the uncertain premise of human supremacy over animals. But are you really the leader, and does your dog know it? Many behavioural problems can occur if you're not the leader. There can be more than one leader in the family, and while children aren't the family leader, they should have the respect of the dog.

Dogs can experience emotional reactions. They experience frustration when they don't know who is in control of their territory and when they don't know which of their actions are acceptable and which are not. Depending on the dog's personality, this uncertainty might manifest itself in the dog's taking over as the leader to the point of growling and snapping or of urinating and defecating in the house after he has been well house-trained.

We feel that it is vitally important for people to understand the leader concept. Establishing the rules of the game can be done easily during puppyhood. It results in a dog that fits into the lifestyle of your home. If minor behavioural problems subsequently arise, they are relatively easy to deal with if you and the dog have developed mutual respect.

The role of leader is abdicated by many people because they see it as the lion-tamer-with-a-whip concept, or as a dictator complex with no pleasant communication allowed. This is not the case at all. In a good dog–person relationship (with you as the dominant member), mutual respect is absolutely necessary. The person must respect the dog and must understand the physical and social needs unique to being a canid. On the other hand, the dog must respect you, and he will if he is treated with consistency and if he knows the rules that you have established are for his benefit. Dogs need guidelines and need to know the limits.

How Do You Become the Leader?

It isn't a short-term battle of wills in which you are the victor and the puppy is vanquished. Leadership is built on daily routine. Being the leader doesn't mean that you must be big and aggressive. A small woman can be the dominant member. It's an attitude – an air of authority. It's the basis for the mutual respect that is so important for building a bridge of communication between the two of you.

> *Dominance isn't power or being aggressive... it's an 'attitude'.*

Many dominance activities are a part of the puppy training routine (which is discussed in detail in Chapter 12). 'Sit' is the most important command that your puppy can learn because it is so easy to use as a reminder that you're in charge. Tell the puppy 'sit' before you feed him, before you play with him, and before you let him go outside. This shows the puppy that he must respond to you before he indulges in pleasure for himself and keeps him from becoming a spoiled brat.

As you're teaching him to sit, praise him with a pat on the chest, which is in itself a means of impressing your leadership position on the puppy. Leaning over is canine language for dominance. (In fact, if you have an especially sensitive or shy puppy you want to avoid leaning over the puppy because it may intimidate him.)

Another good leader exercise involves combining the come with taking the puppy on a walk without a leash. For this, you should take the puppy to an area that's uncrowded, preferably a greenbelt area with no people at all or, in the off-season, a fenced tennis court. Most three-month-old puppies won't want to get too far away from you, which is another reason why this is a good age. Go for a walk together, and when the puppy gets about 3–6 m (10–20 ft) away, get his attention by calling his name and clapping your hands. When he looks at you, kneel down and call him to you. Give him lots of praise when he gets to you and continue your walk, repeating this another three or four times. If you have an independent puppy that ignores you, try running away from him. Many puppies can't resist that and will follow. If you have a very independent puppy, begin

Sit is the most important command your dog learns.

calling him when he's no more than 2.5 m (8 ft) away and give him a small piece of cheese or some other good treat as soon as he comes to you. This exercise reminds the puppy that you're always there and that you're the leader who must be reported to every so often.

You'll be accepted as the family leader by your dog when you're consistent and fair in your demands. For example, if you let the puppy jump up on you one day and the next day you kick or slap him for doing the same thing, the puppy will be confused and will wonder when he can do something and when not.

The family leader doesn't permit the puppy to growl or snap at him. A time out is necessary when this happens, followed by no attention from you for ten to 15 minutes. A growl or a snap is not unusual behaviour for many puppies. It's a natural way for them to show irritation. A loud 'no' and a firm 'sit' lets your puppy know he's in the doghouse. However, if you don't correct the puppy, you're asking for big trouble later. Give some thought as to what stimulus provoked the growl or the snap. If the puppy has been treated unnecessarily roughly, it's up to you to change the situation.

How Does a Dog Become the Leader?

Very easily. He's either ignored most of the time or overindulged and smothered with attention. He isn't trained. He isn't taught the difference between good and bad and so he establishes his own criteria with himself as the centre of attention. As a result, he may become not very pleasant for you or your friends and neighbours to live with. It's supposed to be the other way around – the dog is living in your world. Someone has to call the shots, and both you and your dog will be happier if it's you.

Conclusion

Guide the puppy to behave the way you want him to from the time you bring him home. Be patient. Behaviour development takes time. If you're relaxed and don't turn every act of your puppy into a major battle, you'll find that having a puppy in the house is one of the most delightful experiences you've ever had and that sharing your house with a mature dog that respects you is deeply rewarding.

CHAPTER 9

The Importance of Personality

Sometimes it's difficult to see your puppy as he really is, rather than as you want him to be. Exuberant, forceful people cannot really believe that their puppy might be a little short of confidence and need morale-boosting. Quiet people have difficulty believing that their puppy is leader-oriented and must have a firm hand and firm voice. Surely, this assertive little puppy will become sweet and gentle any day now – wishing will make it so. The fact is, you must accept the puppy the way he is and then proceed to mould the kind of adult dog you want.

Individual Characteristics

The puppy's individual genetic qualities determine factors such as the degree of shyness or aggressiveness and other traits such as curiosity and excitability. These traits are found in all breeds, purebred and mongrel alike, and are components in a dog's personality. What is the basic temperament of your puppy? Is he dependent, independent, leader-oriented, aggressive, eager to please, shy or too easily excited? As the pack leader, you will continue to develop a communication with your puppy by training him. This needs to be done according to the puppy's personality, however, or the training can do more harm than good at this age.

*Accept your puppy as he is,
then mould the kind
of dog you want.*

A dependent puppy can grow into a self-confident adult.

The Dependent Puppy

This puppy is usually found in the toy breeds. He looks to his owner for approval for all of his actions and tends to be emotional. This puppy wants constantly to stay very close to his owner and does a minimum of investigating. It's very easy to get in the habit of carrying this puppy, an activity that should be limited because it will exaggerate the dog's dependency to the extent of making him overly nervous. Gentleness is needed in living with this puppy. Keep showing the puppy what you expect him to do, and he'll soon respond. Don't treat this pup like a baby. That will make him an emotional cripple. Just because he's small and acts very dependent upon you doesn't mean that he can't learn good puppy behaviour.

The Independent Puppy

A little independence is a good thing. There is nothing wrong with having a puppy that thinks for himself at times, but some puppies are more inclined this way than others. The sign of a very independent puppy is to not be able to get his attention to come to you when you call him from only 2 m (6 ft) away. This puppy will ignore your voice and your hand clapping and will sniff along, going his own merry way. If this puppy isn't given puppy training, he will be difficult

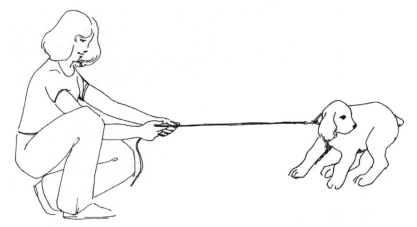

Use a leash to keep the independent puppy from wandering off during your training sessions.

to train as an adult because by then his desire to please will be focused mostly on himself. This puppy takes patience and firmness but generally is easy to train because he is calm and not emotional.

If it's possible, keep the puppy in a dog crate or in a room or garden area by himself for at least 30 minutes before each training session. This will help to encourage his attention to be on you during the session. If at first he seems more interested in everything else than in you, be patient and show him firmly what you want him to do. Reward him with a pat on the chest or with your voice, saying, 'good dog', or both. You may want to use titbits to get his attention. The trick is to keep his attention zeroed in on you. Keep sessions short and be aware that it might take many sessions before your puppy responds the way you want him to.

The Eager-to-Please Puppy

This puppy will respond to your voice very quickly and will eagerly come running to you when you call him (from close distances, of course). It will seem as though he learns very quickly because he wants to do whatever you show him. He's so responsive to you that it's easy to mistake this and think that he already knows how to sit or come or stay. However, this puppy needs much repetition and will take almost as long to actually learn something as the more independent puppy. These puppies are filled with charm and will train you readily to their desires, so watch for this. The eager-to-please puppy is probably the easiest type to work with. Training sessions can be for longer periods without stressing this puppy. However, to begin with, no puppy should have more than five minutes of lessons at one time.

The Shy Puppy

This puppy has some distinctive behavioural patterns. He may crouch and freeze when you approach him. He may be overly sensitive. He may cringe and stay away if you raise your voice even a little. He may be very fearful in a new place, even though there are no noises or other frightening things. He may not

want to approach another person even though the person is quiet and non-frightening. Some puppies will roll on their sides or urinate when you show them attention. This is also an indication of excessive submission.

Guide this puppy gently but firmly to do what you want him to do. Follow a couple of minutes of working with a short play period. Improvement will be slow, but it will come. The puppy may not want to participate in learning any

This puppy shows signs of submissiveness and shyness.

of the commands such as sit or come or stay, but keep repeating the learning sessions with lots of patience.

You must be the pack leader for this puppy also. If you're not, the puppy will take over the job. He can see that he has you trained to let him act the way he wants. For example, if you feel sorry for this puppy when he starts to act shy and frightened and begin to pet him, you are rewarding his behaviour and encouraging him to act that way in the future. Instead, when he begins to act shy, speak to him in a pleasant, firm voice, but don't pet him until his behaviour is more what you want it to be, even if for only a split second. It is especially important to make the training sessions fun. Keep his mind on you and off himself.

The Dominant Puppy

The dominant puppy is a very active one and demands a lot of attention. He's little and cute, and it's very easy to give him all of the attention that he wants. He becomes spoilt because of the overindulgence and, as he grows older, aggressive tendencies might show up and you won't want to cater to him anymore. He will let you know that he's unhappy with you. For example, a competitive puppy might snap at you if you reach down to move his feed dish while he's eating, or he may snap at you during leash training if he decides that he doesn't want to stay at your side. In other words, the puppy will try to do things his way and, if you permit this, you are setting yourself up for serious, difficult behaviour as he gets older. Aggressive actions in the puppy cannot be permitted. We can't stress strongly enough the importance of not allowing the aggressive puppy to become the dominant member of the relationship.

When the puppy snaps at you, it will be a shock and a surprise, but don't retreat, because this is what he wants. This rewards his snapping and

A dominant puppy will demand all the attention.

encourages him to do it again. If this type of puppy were to be slapped as a disciplinary measure, he might take it as a challenge and fight back. Instead, basic obedience training is essential for the leader-oriented puppy. It teaches him that he receives a reward for obeying or submitting to your commands. Teach the puppy the sit command and use it constantly. This keeps reminding the puppy that you're the boss.

The Extremely Excitable Puppy

All puppies can become excited easily, but some won't calm down. Some you can hardly touch because they are constantly wiggling. Such a puppy will really try your patience. He's difficult to work with because you can't get his attention for more than a few seconds. You may need to start with sessions that are less than a minute long. They can gradually become longer as the puppy learns to pay attention. Try not to add to his excitement by any quick motions on your part. Stay calm, with as little body movement as possible. Keep repeating the training routine. Don't pet the puppy or tell him that he's a good dog until you've finished the training session. Sometimes it helps if the puppy is allowed to run off some of his energy in a supervised enclosure before the training lesson begins. Then put the leash on and tell him that school is in session.

If over a period of time you've done the training routine every day and still see no improvement, there may be a psychological reason for the puppy's behaviour. In a few cases, puppies are so excitable that you can't hold their attention long enough to even begin training. These are signs of over-excitability, in which case you should get the help of a vet. Certain dogs have a problem similar to hyperactive children and respond to similar treatment. If you think that this might be the case, discuss it with your vet.

The Trainer's Personality

Your personality is also a factor in puppy training. If you are very shy – or quite assertive – this may indeed affect your puppy's reactions to you. Be aware of how you are coming across to your puppy. If necessary, moderate your approach. Usually, though, a puppy will adjust to your individual personality and will want to do things your way as long as you're consistent and he knows what you want him to do. Within the bounds of respecting your puppy and not abusing him, your method of dog training should be what seems natural to you. It's up to you to decide if you're being too tough on your puppy, or too lenient.

As different as breed and genetic characteristics might be in a population of puppies, almost any one of them, if given adequate socialisation, can learn to respond to humans in a very satisfactory way.

Be honest with yourself. Open your eyes. Your puppy is continually telling you how things really are and what kind of training he needs from you. Puppy training is a one-on-one proposition. Trust your instincts. Listen to your puppy; read his body language. He can tell you a lot more than your neighbour can.

CHAPTER 10

Dog Signals Using Body Language

As your puppy grows into a mature dog, you will see him using many more body language signals than the typical ones we are familiar with. Not only does a dog use his tail and ears and voice to communicate, he uses calming signals and warning signals inherited from his ancestor, the wolf. The signals that domestic dogs use have the same basic meaning as the wolf's signals. But because the world of the dog is so different from the wilderness world of the wolf, dog signals vary in degree or intensity and have a broader meaning. Turid Rugaas, a trainer who gives seminars on dog behaviour throughout the world, has studied these signals for a number of years and written a book on the subject, *On Talking Terms with Dogs: Calming Signals*.

Dogs use calming signals to prevent problems between people and dogs and between themselves and other dogs. Sometimes, dogs use these signals to calm themselves when they feel uneasy about being approached by an unknown person or dog. Calming signals can also be a gesture of goodwill – to make friends, both with other dogs and with people.

Another way dogs use these signals is to calm you when you use a harsh tone of voice, show impatience or communicate with your body language that you are stressed.

Dogs use their bodies to calm themselves, their owners or other dogs and also use warning signals to inform others when they come too far into their space.

Watch your puppy carefully so you can understand dog language. Sometimes a dog's signal is so quick you miss it. Many of the signals involve only slight movements of the head, eyes, lips, tongue or eyebrows.

Because the breeds that exist today have many different physical characteristics, not all dogs can use all the signals. Flop ears, cropped ears, flat muzzles, hair growing over the eyes, no tails or very short tails are reasons that some signals can't be done by some dogs or seen by others. Other dogs are out of practice; they never have an opportunity to use these signals because they never leave their house or garden.

Signals are activated by instinct, but if no opportunity comes along with other dogs or if signals are ignored by people, the signals get weaker or stop altogether. Some breeds use signals more commonly than other breeds. Also, there are differences between individuals within a breed. But the more you watch, the more you can catch a glimpse into the wild heritage of your canine friend.

Calming Signals

Head Turning

This is an obvious and commonly used signal. Some dogs will turn their heads when a rambunctious dog approaches, to slow him down. A good place to watch for this is at a park or in a no-leash area.

ILLUSTRATION © TERRY NASH

A dog will turn his head if he feels uncomfortable or vulnerable. For instance, a Springer Spaniel in obedience class turned his head away from his person every time she leaned over to praise and pet him. Then he would be slow, hesitating to do the next class activity. By turning his head, he was telling this person that he felt frightened by her display of dominance over him. The instructor suggested that the woman stop leaning over her dog and instead reach out with her arm to pat him on his neck or shoulder. His response to this change was to become a happy partner with her in the class.

Head turning can indicate the dog feels uncomfortable.

Turning the Body Sideways to Another Dog

This is a stronger signal. A dog will do this when another dog, often a younger one, gets too rowdy in play. The older dog could also add an additional strong calming signal, **sniffing intensely** at the same spot on the ground, like looking for a treat.

ILLUSTRATION © TERRY NASH

A dog may turn his body sideways as a calming signal to another dog.

When you call your puppy and he not only comes slowly but in a wide curve, you might get angry because you think he's doing this just to irritate you. Actually, he's using two other calming signals. How were you calling him? Did you get excited when he didn't come immediately? These signals, **a curved line** and **slow approach**, were his way of calming you.

Lip Licking

This is a relatively common but not often noticed form of greeting. With many dogs, it's a flicking of the lips. Other dogs, especially black dogs, lick on their noses. You can't miss it. Facial expressions on black dogs don't show very well and therefore they exaggerate with the tongue. You will see this signal when you greet and pet a dog that doesn't know you or when someone new greets your dog. The dog wants to signal that he won't growl or bite, or, if he is sensitive, he will use this as a calming signal for his own nervousness. After you have observed lip licking in various dogs, you will begin to be aware of the message the dog is sending.

Lip licking isn't always a greeting. You might see your puppy licking his lip when he approaches you if you're sick, or if you have just shouted at him. This is a calming signal to him. Molly, a Shih Tzu (a breed developed in China), visited an elderly man in his wheelchair. It had been a long time since he'd held a dog. When Molly was lifted into his lap she looked up at Bill and began lip licking. When he began to pet her, she settled into his lap, no longer using her calming signal.

ILLUSTRATION © TERRY NASH

Lip licking may be a greeting or it may be a calming signal.

The Yawn

The yawn is a signal you can't miss. Most people think it means a dog is bored, but it also has other meanings. It can be an expression of insecurity or embarrassment. Between dogs, it can be used to show friendliness, such as a dominant dog to a submissive one. For example, you might see a yawn when you're teaching your puppy to walk on a leash or to stay. If you expect him to learn more quickly than he is able to, your impatience and tone of voice cause him to feel confused. When you relax, use a pleasant voice, and show him what

ILLUSTRATION © TERRY NASH

Yawning has several meanings. You must look at the situation in order to interpret it correctly.

to do, he becomes more confident of what you want from him, and the need for a yawn disappears.

Lip licking and yawning together can have any one of several meanings, *so how do you know which one a dog is communicating?* Think about the circumstances of the signal – what the dog is doing, what is going on at the time. The more you observe dog signals, the better you will understand them and the better you will understand your puppy or your neighbours' dogs.

Using Calming Signals

You can use some of the signals dogs use with each other. When you see an excited or shy dog walking towards you, turn your head and begin walking towards him in a curved line. When you get closer, ask if you can pet him, approaching him from the side. If you're playing with a dog or puppy that gets too rambunctious, turn your side or your back, fold your arms and don't look at the dog for a minute. This should calm him.

If you're trying to read and your puppy keeps pestering you, try yawning. Some dogs will begin to calm down after only a few yawns. If you see no effect after eight or ten yawns, it's not working. Try again another time.

Warning Signals

When a dog feels his space has been invaded, he sends out warning signals. These are very clear. The first signal of discomfort might be to lower the ears. Another danger signal that the dog is uncomfortable is turning the head, lowering the shoulders. Then the dog might crouch down and try to crawl away.

If these signals are ignored, the result could be a snap, or even a serious bite.

The lips, ears and tail can be used as warning signals to stay away. These are easy to recognise. Have you seen a dog curl his lip? It's usually the front and a corner of the lip. This is often used as a warning to another dog to stay away; the dog won't share his bone. If a dog growls at a member of his people pack, it's a sign that he thinks he's the leader of the pack or wants to be. He needs obedience training so he can learn who's top dog. If a dog's ears are leaning back he's worried; if they are back against his head, he's fearful. If cornered, he could be a fear biter. If the ears are stiff and forward, he's feeling aggressive, ready to fight another dog.

PHOTO © JUDITH STROM

Puppies say they're happy to be with you by licking your face.

Conclusion

Reading a dog's body language is helpful – and fun. Whether you know the dog or he is a stranger, understanding what he's telling you is a good feeling. A dog reads every little bit of our body language; we can learn to read his body language as well. When you watch closely enough to learn what he's telling you with his body, you and your dog really become partners.

Solving Behavioural Problems

Dogs must be taught how to behave. The dog is an intelligent animal capable of learning what actions are not acceptable. The prey instinct is a natural part of all dogs, as it is with the wolf. If a dog is never allowed to participate in prey-instinct activities, he can become overactive, easily excitable or impatient, and substitute such actions as fence running in the garden or barking constantly. Have you ever noticed how a dog that has been where he could run free, follow a scent of a mouse or rabbit, or just sniff different scents comes home in a calm state of mind, often sleeping and woofing and moving his legs as if he's running? This is because he's had some vigorous exercise, but it's also because he has used his prey instinct. The dog's natural drive to imitate a hunt eases the frustration of not always being able to follow his instincts.

You can begin now to head off potential bad habits caused by the puppy's uncontrolled instincts. No matter how comfy a puppy's life is, we will never be able to take the prey instinct totally out of his mind or his behaviour, and we probably don't want to. It is a part of his natural being. Helping him express this in acceptable ways helps us, too. We are working with him in our world, allowing him to keep his dogness in our world.

*Don't let your puppy learn bad habits!
That's the cardinal
rule of the right start.*

You have probably noticed that your puppy has certain behavioural problems in which he specialises. Some puppies seem to have a preference regarding where or how they want to channel their mischief. In this chapter, we will talk about ideas for dealing with specific puppy behaviours that you want to stop. You can and should expect your puppy to learn good behaviour!

Why Is My Puppy Acting this Way?

Most behavioural problems are caused by boredom and isolation. This is why we say that it is essential to spend time every day with your puppy and have him with you in the house or in the garden while you're at home. When you're not at home, the puppy should not be loose but should be either in a crate, in a small puppy-proof room or in an outdoor pen.

The importance of the family pack becomes clear as you note the behaviour problems that can result from the puppy not knowing his position in the pack as he grows up, not knowing who the pack leader is and not having anyone teach him good behaviour.

A few problem behaviours don't become noticeable until the puppy reaches adolescence. By that time, it's more difficult to deal with the problem than it would have been to prevent it earlier. When problem behaviours do appear in earlier puppyhood, start dealing with them right away, because in all probability, they will just get worse. Fortunately, strategies for preventing problems involve very little time and are easily incorporated into activity time that you would already be spending with your puppy.

Guarding the Food Dish

Growling or snapping when someone reaches for the dog's food dish is one of the behaviours that come directly from the pack instinct. The dog doesn't know who's in charge, so he thinks he must be. All family members should work on the food-dish exercise at one time or another. This exercise not only prevents your puppy from becoming protective of his food, it also accustoms him to having hands come close to his face. This is important if there are children in the family.

There are three things that you can do while your puppy is eating. Begin by putting titbits into his dish, one at a time, until he's accustomed to your hand reaching out towards his dish. The treat should be something special, such as small pieces of sausage, cheese or cooked chicken. You want him to associate a hand in his food dish with something very pleasant. After he has become very comfortable with your hand in his dish, touch his dish, moving it out of position. Finally, pick up his dish and set it back down. If your puppy is starting to guard his toys, offer a titbit while you take his bone or toy from him. This conditions him to accepting your hand. If he growls at any time, use a vinegar squirt bottle and give a 'no!'

Conditioning your puppy to hands in his food bowl prevents growling and guarding of his food when he matures.

Sooner or later your puppy will find a slipper to chew.

Jumping out of Reach

It's very natural for a puppy to scoot out of reach when you bend over to take him by the collar. Use a yummy titbit for this also. Whenever you call your puppy to you, give him a treat with one hand while the other hand touches his collar. In this way, he'll be comfortable with your hand reaching for his collar. Be sure that your puppy comes all the way to you before he receives his treat – don't reach out to him.

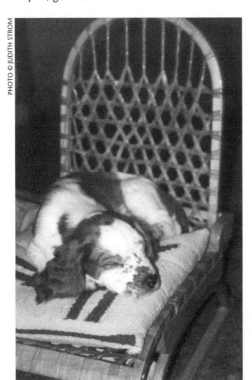

PHOTO © JUDITH STROM

Let your puppy learn that he can be comfortable by himself and you may head off separation anxiety.

Separation Distress

Conditioning your puppy to being left home alone can prevent serious problems. If not attended to, separation distress can develop into separation anxiety, which is often expressed by frantic barking and destructiveness. In extreme cases, this destructiveness can involve furniture and even walls and doors. Conditioning your puppy to being left at home alone can avoid these problems arising when your puppy grows older. We periodically meet with dog owners who have this problem. It could have been avoided by dealing with this distress when the puppy was young, which is the easy time to work with it. By the time a dog reaches adolescence, it is a serious problem indeed.

If your puppy has had constant attention since he first arrived at your home, and then you suddenly leave him at home alone, he can experience a state of isolation that results in fear and panic. Therefore, you need to help your puppy learn to be comfortable by himself. Teaching the puppy that it's okay to be alone should be done while you're at home, too. If the puppy is to be left in a small room or the back garden while you're gone, put him there occasionally while you're at home working around the house.

Begin with short separation periods of five minutes. If he's barking when you're ready to return to him, try to wait until he has stopped (at least long enough to take a breath), then open the door. Gradually increase the length of time before you return.

The manner in which you leave the house and later return to your puppy is also a factor in how he perceives your absence. If you're emotional and feel guilty about leaving him, he'll sense this and will become nervous and upset. Practise your arrivals and departures at the same time you're conditioning him to your absence. When you leave him, don't be emotional – no petting or special fun games. Such handling followed immediately by separation can result in more intense separation distress. Keep your departure low-key. You can speak to your puppy and tell him that you're leaving, then leave. Use the same phrase every time you leave, for example, 'Be a good dog; I'll be back'. When you arrive home, greet your puppy warmly but briefly and go about your business. Later, when you have time, you can have a play period, take a walk or whatever.

If your absences are occasional and are for no more than a few hours at a time, the puppy's crate is ideal and should not result in distress because that's his den and he is accustomed to it. But all puppies should be taught that they can stay at home alone for longer periods of time. Try to have a larger safe area for your puppy if you'll be gone longer than a few hours. Make sure that there's a place where he can eliminate and a cosy shelter in case of bad weather if he's outdoors.

Digging

There's no magic answer here. It's not your puppy's fault that you have a perfectly landscaped garden. Sniffing and digging in the dirt are naturally doggy things to do, especially for puppy dogs. If you can't be out with the puppy all the time to distract him when he begins digging, fix a fenced area where he is free to dig all he desires. When you see him digging in another part of the lawn, take him to his own area. Some puppies will learn to like digging in their own place, especially if there's a hole already started or the ground is soft or you've planted a bone. Most puppies outgrow digging, but some mature dogs will periodically dig all their lives. The earth is cool, and burying bones is a strong impulse with them. Boredom is another cause of continuing digging.

> *DIG • CHEW*
>
> *Understanding how natural instincts can still have their place will make both you and puppy happier.*
>
> *GUARD • JUMP*

Chewing

Puppies chew for three reasons: they are bored and want something to do, they have too much energy from not enough exercise, and/or they are teething and have sore gums. You will need to teach your puppy that chewing on his own toys is the only chewing allowed. This is the process that we call moulding your puppy's behaviour and is discussed in a previous chapter. For many puppies, this keeps problem chewing to a minimum; however, there's always an item or two around the house that they can't resist, and there is also that percentage of puppies that are exceptionally mouthy.

Puppies need to learn that chewing on their own toys is the only chewing allowed.

For problem chewers, a bad taste often inhibits the chewing desire. Try Bitter Apple, available in pet supply shops, or try very hot Chinese or Mexican pepper sauce. Listerine and its aroma can be a repellent to puppies. (Test the furniture or other pieces with a small amount to be certain that no discolouration occurs.) Puppies are very sensitive to a distasteful substance and should quickly associate that with the item to which it has been applied. Keep applying the substance until the puppy is no longer testing the area to see if the taste has changed. Be consistent!

Puppies are at their worst during the teething process between four to six months of age, but the problem can continue periodically for several more months. Some puppies find relief by chewing an ice cube or a frozen rawhide chip. To avoid serious chewing damage, never give your puppy the run of the house. He should either be with you so that you can monitor his chewing, or he should be confined. Tether the puppy to you with a leash or other cord. Then he can be with you when you're too busy to keep track of him all the time. Too many valuables have been ruined because the puppy's owner wanted to be 'nice'.

Barking

Some of the herding and terrier breeds have been bred to increase their barking as part of their job. Other dogs of any breed bark because of loneliness and isolation. Spending every day alone stresses many dogs and they begin to bark. They keep on barking and it becomes a habit.

Now is the time to develop a pattern of control for barking. This is probably one of the most frustrating problems facing a dog owner. It can create enemies of neighbours and can result in warnings and fines from local authorities – and justifiably so. Any dog that won't stop barking for long periods of time is causing much distress for numerous innocent people and is contributing to anti-dog sentiment. The responsible dog owner avoids this problem from the start by teaching her puppy the quiet command.

Barking is a natural canine activity. There's no reason to expect a dog never to bark, but you can expect him to learn to stop barking. The shake can is a good way to accomplish this. When the puppy has barked a few times, give the quiet command, then shake the can until the barking stops. The noise should startle the puppy into silence, at which point you immediately praise him! The puppy will probably begin barking again, and you will repeat the procedure as many times as necessary until the puppy doesn't return to barking. Always give the command first, then the distraction. Always praise the puppy as soon as he stops barking.

You also might want to attract him away from where he is barking so that you can achieve success with the quiet command. This is an ongoing process. Some puppies learn the quiet command quickly, while others have regular relapses. As with many other aspects of puppy behaviour, you automatically work on the problem every time it occurs until you reach a point where you say, 'Wow, he's learning that command really well!'

The puppy that is barking outside at night shouldn't be left out all night. He should be in the house, in a crate or in a secure area. The cause of some barking problems is similar to the cause of some excessive chewing and digging problems – not enough time spent with the puppy and not enough exercise for him.

Jumping Up

One serious behavioural problem is when the puppy – or the dog – jumps on or chases children. Young children have an erratic gait, which can trigger an automatic chase response in the dog's brain. Therefore, he must be taught that this is forbidden. The off command (which means to keep all feet off humans) can be used for this. Use it consistently whenever the puppy tries to jump on anybody. Eventually, the off command, when used at an appropriate time, will stop the puppy before he jumps.

You need to help your puppy understand what this command means. The isolation method works well for this. When he jumps on you, say, 'Off!' Then turn away and fold your arms across your chest, totally ignoring the puppy. Continue to ignore him if he jumps again, and again. Don't look at him. When he stops jumping up, relax and praise him. Repeat the isolation immediately if he jumps again. Also, give him pats and praise when he's with you and not jumping.

To teach the puppy about jumping on children, have the puppy on his leash, or make a 3 m (10 ft) line out of clothesline or other cord. This ensures that you will have instant control for correcting your puppy's behaviour. Set aside a time for this activity during a play period. When your child comes close and the puppy starts to run and jump, give the off command, followed by a quick tug on the leash. Praise him as soon as he is being good. If he immediately jumps up, repeat the correction and then the praise.

Continue the training even after your puppy begins to understand and is seldom jumping up. Many repetitions are necessary before the puppy learns to inhibit this instinct. You need to repeat this set-up for several days in succession and again weekly for a period of time. The child must also be taught how to behave – no screaming or shouting or waving arms around.

Mouthiness and Biting

These actions are normal for puppies. His mother and littermates were the first teachers to tell him not to do this. His people must teach him it's not acceptable at any time.

A dog feels the world through his mouth. The mouth – the teeth, the cheeks and the tongue – is a tactile area. If you watch a mature dog, you might see him mouth an item to identify it or understand it. With your puppy, this natural tendency can sometimes get out of hand. Now that the puppy is living in your pack, you replace the interaction that the puppy would have had with the other puppies and dogs. You must step in and continue with bite-inhibition training in a manner that is perceived as normal by your puppy.

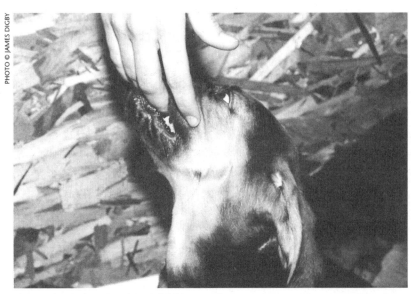

PHOTO © JAMES DIGBY

This puppy is learning bite inhibition or the easy command – not to bite down when a hand is placed in his mouth.

Trading a treat for a toy prevents snapping in the future. Return the toy within a few seconds.

Teach your puppy the stop-it or no-bite command. When he nips at you, take him by the collar and look him in the eye for several seconds while you repeat the command. Release him and in a few seconds tell him quietly that he's a good puppy. Reach out to touch him, and if he starts playing with his mouth again, repeat the correction.

Another effective correction is to isolate the puppy – totally ignore him as soon as you say 'no bite!' Fold your arms, and don't even look at him. After a couple of minutes, give your puppy another chance to play with you. Repeat the isolation routine as often as necessary until he moderates his mouthiness.

Occasionally, a puppy owner needs to wear a glove to help teach the puppy about biting. With a glove, you can keep your hand movements slow and calm. Often it is the jerky hand movements (jerky because of his sharp teeth) that excite the puppy and keep him grabbing the hand in play.

The glove can also be used to teach your puppy the easy or the gentle command so that you can put your hand in the puppy's mouth and he won't bite down. *All puppies must learn this command, whatever their breed.*

The Aggressive Puppy

Occasionally, there is a puppy that bites not in play but out of fear or dominance aggression. This demands a big 'no!' with your voice. The swiftness of the correction is imperative. Do not talk to the puppy after this correction for several minutes.

In the adult dog, aggression is the single most serious behavioural problem vets and trainers encounter. It's normal for a puppy to have an aggressive reaction to some action that he perceives as threatening to him.

However, we emphasised previously that early socialisation is very important in familiarising your puppy with the variety of circumstances that he will encounter in life. If your puppy has had a well-balanced relationship with his littermates until weaning, this bodes well for his ability to interact with dogs in the future. If your puppy has been handled kindly by you and by other members of the family – young and old, male and female – this bodes well for future transactions with people. Subsequently, as the puppy passes through the period of environmental awareness (nine to 12 weeks), his understanding of dominance and submission is enhanced. He becomes increasingly aware of his environment and really begins to appreciate what a nice person you are. Finding and establishing the right balance of dominant and submissive behaviour throughout these stages will result in a more confident and socially well-adjusted puppy. These are the puppies that will be less likely to give you problems with aggressive behaviour. In fact, many of the early problems with fear and dominance-cued aggression will be reduced or prevented by your diligently following the full socialisation programme.

The puppy must learn that any aggressive act will be totally inhibited. Certain cues, such as rapid movement of hands towards the puppy, can elicit an aggressive response. These puppies must be conditioned to hand movement immediately. With a titbit in one hand, let the puppy nibble and lick while the other hand moves towards the puppy's ear. If the puppy stops nibbling and eyes the hand, move the hand back. Keep moving forward with one hand (the other is holding the titbit in front of the puppy's mouth) until you can scratch behind the ear and pet the puppy. Then reverse hands and repeat the same procedure. At this point, it is essential to teach the gentle, or easy, command, beginning with a gloved hand and progressing to putting your bare hand in the mouth. If this isn't done during the puppy months, very serious problems lie ahead. In addition, puppy training is essential for this puppy. This builds self-confidence in the fearful puppy and develops an appropriate relationship with the dominant puppy.

PHOTO © MEGGIN RUTHERFORD

When your puppy looks at you while walking on a loose leash, praise him for being a good puppy. Don't wait until he ignores you and pulls on the leash.

Find Creative Solutions

No book can possibly cover all of the various and unique problems that puppies present. As you get to know your puppy, you will learn what types of disciplines are most effective for him, as well as what types of distractions work best. You can utilise this knowledge to determine your own ideas for behavioural problems. Adolescent puppies can certainly keep us on our toes when it comes to staying one jump ahead of their busy minds.

Perhaps your puppy is jumping up and getting things off the kitchen counter. You need to stop this behaviour immediately. If you can catch him at it the first times he tries it, your chances of extinguishing the behaviour are very good. Use your imagination and think of a set-up that will startle him. For example, put some food on a piece of newspaper on the counter. Stack some empty tins around the back and sides of the food. When his paws get on the counter, the paper will move, which will send the tins tumbling. At the same time, you're going to appear from behind a door, saying, 'No! Off!' After he's been impressed with the results of his behaviour, you can tell him that you much prefer him to keep all of his feet on the floor, and that he's a good boy when he does that.

Teaching your puppy the rules of the house is an ongoing, day-by-day process. The weeks of teaching good manners can be very rewarding as you watch the puppy blossom with a sense of confidence. The weeks will also be filled with humour and good times, and the occasional times of total frustration will be kept to a minimum.

Here's a suggestion. When you do reach a point of frustration, give some thought to the various aspects of the puppy's irritating behaviour. Where do your actions fit in? Your puppy is acting in accordance with his dog genes. It's your responsibility to understand this and to understand his need for consistency in your behaviour. After all, you're the mature, reasoning individual in this growing relationship – *aren't you?*

CHAPTER 12

The Rewards of Puppy Training

Just as mature dogs show their puppies how to pay attention and how to behave in the pack, so now the human must show the puppy how to pay attention and behave as a new member of the human pack. This is puppy training – teaching a puppy how to be a happy, co-operative member of his human pack.

You may think this training isn't necessary for your puppy. He's so attentive and does everything that you want him to do. Please, take it on faith that he needs to learn the basics of how to concentrate and how to do basic tasks on command while it's still easy for you both. When your puppy is around six months of age and older, he'll want to do what he wants to do and when he wants to do it. If you have a communication system going by then, you'll be able to minimise some of the major frustrations he'll devise, such as running through the house, jumping on people and furniture, tracking every interesting smell and, most of all, ignoring you. Female puppies are just as good at this as males.

The single most important factor in raising and training a puppy from three to six months of age is getting the puppy to pay attention to you.

Communicating with Your Puppy

The tasks that you teach in puppy training are the foundation for communication as your puppy ventures into adolescence. You want to bring out the best in your puppy. You want him to relate to you, to your family, to your vet and to your friends. The basis for a relationship between you and your puppy is built through the use of your hands, your eyes, your voice and the leash.

Using Your Hands

The puppy's first contact with human hands is in the whelping box, where he is picked up and handled as part of the daily routine – with a certain amount of cuddling, too. These hands move with confidence, and the stroking gives the puppy a feeling of security.

After you take the puppy to your home, your hands will calm the puppy, warm him, play with him and let him know that he can have confidence in his new pack home. However, as the pack leader, you must take care that his attitude towards hands doesn't change. Hands sometimes come at the puppy too often and too abruptly (especially if there are children in the family), and the puppy might growl or snap or shy away. To prevent this, you can teach your puppy that hands are okay, that even though the movement might be quick and startling, these are human hands and should be accepted as a fact of life. You are also responsible for seeing that the puppy is never abused by hands.

The way in which you use your hands during the puppy's socialisation determines how that puppy will react to your hands. He has to learn how to read your hand movements. To begin conditioning your puppy to hand movements, use tiny titbits. Have them in your pocket, and occasionally when your puppy is close to you, offer a titbit. While he is sniffing and taking it, reach out for his collar with your other hand, or touch his ear or pat him on the head. As he gets accustomed to take titbits, move your hand more quickly. Each member of the family should do this individually.

When you begin teaching basic commands such as the sit, become very aware of where your hand is. Does it stay in the appropriate position, or does it wave about randomly as although the hand muscles are not under your control? Many of you will be surprised to find how erratic your hand movements are – over and around and anywhere but next to the puppy's lips and nose – which is where your hand should be when you begin the teaching process. Any other movement can be distracting or confusing to the puppy. The details of hand position and movement will be discussed in the instructions for teaching the various tasks.

Above: Continue to use voice and hand communication as your puppy matures. Keep his attention on you. Use your voice. Pat your leg. Offer a treat.

Below: Get your puppy's attention the moment he becomes distracted.

PHOTO © MEGGIN RUTHERFORD

The 'watch me' command focuses your puppy's attention on you.

Using Your Eyes

Eye contact in the wolf pack is one of the ways of keeping order. Only the alpha animals (male and female) use it, to remind the others of who's in charge and, in general, to maintain the status quo of the leader. To a certain extent, this is also the purpose for human–dog eye contact. When you initiate eye contact, you express your alpha position. The difference is that you don't expect your puppy to turn away or avert his eyes. You should encourage your puppy to maintain eye contact for several seconds, and you should make the contact a pleasant experience.

Use the term 'watch me' or use the puppy's name to teach eye contact. You can make a noise to get his attention, wiggle your fingers up beside your eye, or move a titbit from his nose to your eye until he understands what you want. Always praise him the instant you have eye contact – that is how he learns what you want. If you have trouble getting your puppy to look at you, take his muzzle (or whole head) in your hands, and turn his head up towards you. Praise him the instant your eyes connect, then release him. A very submissive dog will have a hard time maintaining eye contact, so give him lots of encouragement. A dominant puppy won't want to make eye contact on your terms, but keep working at it and praise him vigorously when he gives you even a momentary glance.

Be calm and confident when you ask for eye contact. Smiling is okay. Stand up straight. You're asking for your puppy's respect, so don't get down on his level for this. Read your puppy's eyes.

Continually use eye contact – in the house, on walks, whenever. The puppy that grows up never having established a pattern of eye contact will become a dog that is not readily trainable, and he will have trouble learning good manners.

The watch me command teaches your puppy that you want his attention – that you want him to check in with you. Therefore, it can be followed by a command such as 'sit', or 'this way', or it can be followed by a 'good dog' and a pat on the head or shoulder. You've attracted your puppy's attention – you're happy and he's happy. As you continue to get eye contact and to keep it for longer than a few seconds, you'll be delighted at your puppy's expressions and at how beautiful his eyes are. That feeling seems to be mutual.

Using Your Voice

Throughout all the other aspects of puppy training, your voice is the one constant – the one prevailing influence on your puppy's basic attitude towards you. The tone of your voice can aid your puppy's blossoming sense of confidence or it can keep him watching you out of the corners of his eyes, wondering when harshness is going to strike again. The opposite of harshness is equally disturbing to a puppy but in a different way. A high-pitched, baby-talk tone of voice can keep a puppy confused. He perceives that as an emotional tone, one similar to early tones of his littermates. We have seen puppy behaviour settle down considerably when the owner slowed down the word flow and lowered her voice.

A growly voice when you're disciplining your puppy, a happy voice when you're praising your puppy and a firm, calm voice when you're training your puppy are all natural, and all make sense to your puppy. He learns to know which tone goes with which of his behaviours, and this knowledge greatly speeds the moulding of his behaviour. This, indeed, is puppy training.

Using the Leash

Most dog owners don't think of the leash as a means of communication. They see it as an item to prevent the puppy from wandering off. But think about this. How much time will your dog, during his life, spend at the other end of the leash? Most of you probably live in communities that have a leash law. Therefore, unless you know of some open space where your dog can run loose (and we hope that you do), your dog will spend a great amount of time walking and running on a leash or on a long line (marvellous for giving the puppy 6–9 m (20–30 ft) of roaming and still keeping him under control).

Your puppy's perception of you is determined in part by the way in which he is treated on the leash. If you're rough and inconsistent with jerks and pulls, your puppy will be confused. In contrast, if your puppy drags you wherever he wishes, he perceives you as letting him do whatever he wants. Neither of these attitudes is a basis for good communication. Look upon your leash as a training tool. The details for doing this are described later in this chapter.

Teaching Your Puppy to Learn

Puppy training isn't obedience training. The object of puppy training is to help your puppy learn how to perform certain tasks, such as sit, come, down and walk on a leash. The tasks themselves have a purpose beyond the performance by the puppy. We use them to teach the puppy how to learn. This means getting all of his neurons sparking in the right order so that, as he matures, he will be able to process the steps of learning and will have the commands (vocabulary) to use as building blocks in learning other activities.

What else do we mean when we say that we are teaching a puppy how to learn? We teach the puppy to look at us, to listen to us and to concentrate for a few seconds. This results in his doing the task and in his receiving praise. The watching, listening and concentrating skills are the skills that your puppy will use all of his life, and they soon will be of great value as the puppy grows into adolescence and becomes more independent. If puppy kindergarten classes are available in your community, we highly recommend this experience for you and your puppy.

Teaching Basic Tasks

Using Titbits

In the morning when you get up, put titbits in your pocket. When you get home from work, put titbits in your pocket. And on days off, keep titbits in your pocket, because you never know when you will be using one. The nice thing about puppy training is that it can be done anywhere at any time.

Guiding your puppy with titbits to sit, to down, to come and to walk beside you is the quickest and most stress-free way to teach your puppy. The valuable part about this type of training is that it teaches your puppy to pay attention to you at the same time that it teaches him to concentrate and to focus his attention on an action. The more he does it, the more he gets praised and the more his confidence grows. A good habit is thus formed.

These titbits should be something that your puppy really likes, not pieces of his dog food. Thinly sliced sausages really get a puppy's attention. Cheese is also popular. Try popcorn with garlic powder sprinkled on it. Various commercial treats are also enticing. It's well worth the effort to find something that your puppy thinks is very exciting. For the puppy that isn't a greedy-guts, you may have to teach him to like a titbit. At mealtime, before you show him his supper, get him excited about the titbit that you're holding and see if he'll take it from your fingers. Toss a piece into his food bowl. All puppies can be convinced that a titbit is a great thing – we've never seen an otherwise uninterested puppy turn down a piece of cooked liver. The exception to using special treats is for the excitable puppy that can't be readily taught to take the titbit without turning somersaults. This puppy can be trained with bits of his regular food.

We think that using titbits is the quickest and easiest way to teach puppies how to learn. Their use, however, must be put in perspective. A titbit is a secondary reward. Your voice is the primary reward. This means that your puppy will learn that your exciting voice and playful pats are especially great because they're immediately followed by a favourite titbit. Gradually, you will stop offering the titbit, and then your voice and enthusiasm will become the puppy's total reward for good behaviour.

Food-following is a good description for introducing the basic tasks to your puppy. You don't want to use a leash unless you are working in an area that is dangerous for an off-leash puppy. At this age, you can usually keep the puppy's attention with your voice, your hands and your body language. You want the puppy to be guided into learning these tasks without the distracting pull and jerk of a leash.

Leash Training

Even though you're going to use food-following as much as possible, your puppy needs to be accustomed to a leash. When you first introduce your puppy to a leash, clip it onto his collar and follow him wherever he goes. Then, with your voice and by patting your hand on your leg, encourage him to follow you for a few steps. Some puppies adjust to a leash immediately while others might need several sessions of just having the leash attached to them. The puppy should wear a comfortable buckle collar – keep checking it for size because puppies grow fast. The leash should be about 2 m (6 ft) long and made of nylon, cotton webbing or leather. A piece of soft clothesline will also get the job done. No chain leashes, please.

The Walk Alongside

Initiate the training by using food-following. A tasty titbit in your hand is the guide for showing your puppy that bouncing along close to your side is a great place to be. This is preferably done with no leash, but if you're in an area where you must have a leash on your puppy, fold it in your right hand until it is comfortably loose as it hangs down from the puppy's collar. If you have your puppy out for a walk, do this exercise a couple of times during the walk, then let the puppy whiz around, sniffing and learning about the world, the rest of the time. Use a command when you begin, such as 'with me' or 'let's go'.

Some Pointers:

- Work the puppy on your left side. (This is not a rigid rule, but being consistent has value.)

- Let the puppy lick and nibble the titbit in your left hand. Talk to him and use his name. After a few training sessions, raise your hand holding the titbit to your waist. Lower it back down in front of his nose whenever he becomes distracted. If he gets a short distance away from you, call him with 'come'. Walk backwards, then give him the titbit when he gets to you. Continue walking forwards.

A yummy treat introduces your puppy to staying at your side.

Raise the treat to your waist but give him a sniff every few seconds.

When your puppy gets to the end of the leash, say 'this way' and walk at an angle away from the puppy. Don't jerk the leash or increase your speed. Let the leash tell the puppy he wasn't paying attention.

When he catches up, praise and give him a treat at your side. Continue this every time you walk and he'll soon learn what 'this way' means. As your puppy grows older, this will be the most effective walking command.

- Move at a pace to keep your puppy trotting or jogging.

- Stop while your puppy is still trotting or jogging. Use lots of happy praise.

- Stop while the puppy is still paying attention to you. Gradually increase the length of time of each heeling. Begin with ten seconds.

- If your puppy wanders off, you don't have his attention. Stop walking in a straight line. Try a different titbit. Run backwards and make quick turns. Go in circles. Give him the titbit and begin again (or stop if he has worked long enough).

- Praise your puppy at the end of each heeling 'trip'. Pat the puppy and use a happy voice.

After your puppy has done numerous food-following walks, have him walk alongside with a leash. The leash should be just long enough to hang down slightly from his collar. As soon as your puppy moves away from you and tightens the leash, give a slight pop on it. This should bring the puppy back to your side (he wasn't very far away) and you can tell him, without slowing down, that he's a 'good dog'. After a minute or two of this kind of leash walking, let him relax and continue his walk with sniffing and trotting. Remember to use the release command, 'okay', when you stop the short leash walking. Use the heel command now if you wish.

If you have a problem with the puppy pulling on the leash, remember the pack instinct and the prey drive. He wants to know what's out there. He has high energy. He needs to know you're in charge.

PHOTO © JAMES DIGBY

If your puppy wanders away, run backwards and call him to you.

Left: To teach your puppy to check in with you, begin by letting him explore. Do not give him a come command.

Right: Gradually pull in the loose line so he won't run off if distracted.

Left: Give him lots of praise and treats when he gets back to you.

Checking In

Food finding is used to teach puppies to check in with their person. Use a long line to keep the puppy from wandering off beyond a certain distance. Let the puppy sniff and walk around. As he comes closer, take up the slack on his line but don't call him or use his name. When he finally gets back to home base, give him a yummy treat and lots of praise. Repeat this exercise in different places several times.

The long line, which can be about 6–9 m (20–30 ft), should be used on walks where the puppy can venture out away from you. At this point, he's familiar with checking in with you for a titbit or praise and does so readily when you call him. Eventually, you'll reach a time and age when you can walk in an area where your dog can be off leash, and he won't just take off and run. He will be accustomed to checking in, with a little verbal help from you.

The retractable lead is a great help for having your dog walk out and return to you. It comes in a variety of lengths, the longest being 8 m (26 ft). You will enjoy the comfort and ease of using one, but it doesn't take the place of a leash. Your puppy must learn manners on a leash, because there are many areas where a leash is best.

Wait

This is a command that you will probably use more often than any other. 'Wait while I open the door', 'Wait while I walk out first', 'Wait while I open the car door', 'Wait while I go out the gate first', 'Wait until that car goes by'. While this command keeps your puppy from leaping and charging around, it also teaches him that you are first to do things, and then it's his turn. For many of these situations, your puppy will be on a leash and you will be able to use little tugs. You can also put your hand in front of his face to remind him and block him with your leg. It takes very little time to do this consistently at every door, so don't allow yourself to be in too much of a hurry, letting your puppy go charging out first. If you are consistent, your puppy will learn quickly.

Tell your puppy to wait. Be ready to step in front of him or tug on the leash if he starts to get ahead of you.

Place

If your puppy has a mat or pad in the room where you entertain friends, watch television, etc., he can learn to go there on command and stay. This will probably take a few weeks of helping him to remember what the place command means. Keep encouraging him, and use the stay command after he knows it.

PHOTO © MEGGIN RUTHERFORD

PHOTO © MEGGIN RUTHERFORD

Notice the position of the hand. If the treat is held even a few centimetres above the nose, the puppy will jump for it instead of sitting.

The Sit

Your puppy is accustomed to your hand, and you'll use hand movement to teach the sit. Hold your hand with the titbit right on top of the puppy's nose. With a wiggly puppy, touch the front of his nose. Say 'sit' while moving your hand back (parallel to the floor, not up). As soon as he sits, say 'good dog' and give him the titbit. Don't expect him to stay there, because he's much too lively for that.

For the puppy that is too bouncy to put his tail on the floor, quickly give a titbit when the puppy's hind legs bend even the slightest amount. You'll be amazed to see a good sit in two or three days. One puppy took a week, but that's the exception. Continue guiding with treats until a snappy sit is consistent. As soon as your puppy will sit on voice command without being guided, give him a titbit for a job well done. Praise him first, then immediately give the titbit. There will come a time when your praise will take the place of the titbit.

The Come

Your hands will be the visual reinforcement of your come command. To begin teaching the command, have both hands close in front of you holding a titbit. With your puppy right there, licking the titbit, walk backwards repeating the come command. After a few steps, give the treat to the puppy and praise him. A few times of doing this is usually sufficient to impress your puppy with the rewards of coming right up to you.

Your come commands can be anywhere in the house or in a fenced garden. No leash is needed for the puppy. Kneel down on the puppy's level. Be sure that he is close to you, looking at you, before you tell him to come. Distance comes much later. Puppies learn fastest when they have success. Use the puppy's name and then the command, 'Tippy, come!' Clap your hands or pat the floor, or both. You'll find that in a month or two, when your puppy is distracted by something or you're farther away, your puppy will respond to your hand movements when he was initially deaf to your voice. Always use them together in the teaching phase.

Gradually increase the distance from your puppy when you call him to you, but not beyond 6–9 m (20–30 ft). If he gets distracted, get his attention back on you, walking closer to him if necessary. When your puppy comes all the way to you for his titbit, touch his collar with your other hand. This helps him to be comfortable with a hand reaching for the collar in the future when you might not have a titbit. Don't grab for the puppy when he's close to you but not completely there. If you do, he'll quickly learn the play-around-just-out-of-reach game that puppies think is such fun.

A reminder (because we all tend to get frustrated at times) – *never scold your puppy once he has finally come*. You needn't praise, but you simply can't show your anger, because that's a sure way to teach your puppy to go in the other direction when you call. Try walking away, or lie down on the ground – your puppy will probably come just because you're ignoring him.

Now it's time to practise the come command in parks and open spaces. For this, you need a long line that you can buy already made, or you can go to a hardware shop and make your own. Choose about 9 m (30 ft) of whatever will be comfortable in your hand when your puppy pulls on it. Buy a small clasp, one that isn't big and heavy, and tie it on. Another good idea is a retractable long line, called a Flexi-Lead, available in pet supply shops. This is the best for both you and your puppy. It takes the pulling pressure off your arms and shoulders, and your dog is always under control. Yet it allows him the liberty of running, sniffing and being a normal dog on a walk.

Take your puppy for a walk. Let him wander around, and when he's interested in sniffing and poking around, call his name. If he doesn't look at you, call his name again and give a quick tug on the line. When he looks at you, praise him immediately and call him to you, giving him a titbit and touching his collar. Then let him run out on his long line again. Call him to check in with you occasionally during the walk. This reinforces the come command even when he's distracted. He gets a titbit before going out again.

The puppy comes all the way to the treat in the hand. If you reach out, he will learn not to come in close.

PHOTO © MEGGIN RUTHERFORD

Above: To teach the down stay, put your foot on the leash close to the clasp of the leash.
Below: When the puppy starts to stand up, the leash reminds him to stay down. If the leash is too long, the puppy will sit. Put him down gently and move your foot closer to the clasp.

The Down Stay

The down command, followed by a stay (which will only be for five to ten seconds at first but gradually works up to a minute), impresses upon your puppy his relationship with you – that you are benevolent and worthy of respect. This is especially important for males or dominant breeds or individuals. For the down, put the titbit right under your puppy's nose (he's sitting), then down to the floor between his feet, and slide it out in front. He should lie down as he follows it. If he doesn't, help him by *gently* pushing down on his shoulders.

After your puppy has learned the down command and is comfortable with it, add the stay command. Put your foot on the leash, close to the clasp, and stand up. The puppy won't be able to stand up because the leash is too short. If he wiggles, he soon finds out that he can't go anywhere and then he lies back down again. He's teaching himself that when you say 'down' and 'stay', he is expected to lie down and stay there. Don't take your foot off the leash until you have released him with your voice. 'Okay, good dog!'

The second step is a down stay with the leash on the floor, but you don't stand on it. You need to be ready to stop the puppy the instant he starts to move. Gradually work up to a minute in time, but continue to stand close to the puppy.

The Sit Stay

The first step is to reach the point where your puppy is comfortable sitting at your side for at least a count of five. You can stroke your puppy, scratching him behind the ears to help him relax and sit still. Do not attempt this exercise before your puppy is 12 weeks of age.

Fold the leash in your left hand so that it is short but doesn't pull. Place your open right hand in front of the puppy's nose. Give the command 'stay'. Step directly in front of your puppy with your toes almost touching the puppy's toes. Count to five, then step back to heel position. Count to three, release and give praise.

A puppy learns to do things in a step-by-step manner. For example, in teaching the sit stay, you must first teach him to stay while you stand toe-to-toe in front of him, then to stay while you're almost a metre in front of him. You must still be able to correct him with a tug on the leash if he starts to move. You then teach him to stay while you walk around him, and again you must be able to correct him with a tug on the leash. Then you work on the exercise while standing about a metre or so in front of him. Many puppies will take several weeks to progress through these steps, but they are necessary if you want to teach the stay effectively.

Some puppies are very wiggly and must learn to sit quietly before you can teach the stay.

Keep the leash a little shorter than this so you can give your puppy an instant cue with a tug on the leash that reminds him to continue sitting.

What you can expect from your puppy

Your training programme will be in the everyday process of living with your puppy. It's your responsibility to insist on your puppy's attention – your puppy's responsibility is to be happy and playful in responding to you. To keep your puppy tuned in to you, continually raise your expectations. As the weeks go by, expect the following behaviours to become consistent.

To concentrate on what he is doing. Begin with a few seconds of your puppy's total attention while he is walking at your side, gradually extending the length of time up to a minute.

To pay attention. The 'watch me' is a good way to reinforce this (and also puts you in the alpha position).

To look towards you when puppy hears his name. Follow through with a 'sit', a 'come', etc., or even just a 'good dog!'

To sit. The control you have by using this command is basic to teaching your dog good manners. After you stop his bad behaviour, insist on a 'sit'. He has then responded to your authority and you praise him for good behaviour.

To come when called – at a short distance off leash, and from a farther distance on a long line. Keep a few titbits in your pocket to reward your puppy when he gets to you.

To lie down and stay there for a short while. This communicates your alpha relationship. Begin with ten seconds, gradually lengthening to one to two minutes.

Clicker Training

Clicker training has become popular in the dog world in recent years. It was first used about 40 years ago in training dolphins and other wild animals. Karen Pryor, a renowned dolphin trainer, was among the first persons to write about this method of positive reinforcement, presenting it in vocabulary and training steps that could be used by people with their own pets. We recommend the video, *Clicker Magic – The Art of Clicker Training*.

A variety of other books on clicker training have also been published and do a fine job of presenting the practical aspects of using a clicker. They will cover the subject in more depth and enable you to expand on the training given here.

Clicker training is operant conditioning (positive reinforcement) where a click is paired with a reward. This motivates a dog to perform a desired physical behaviour. It's not for everyone. Your dog isn't on leash. You don't give any command initially, and you must watch carefully for the movement you want, clicking at the precise moment the dog is in the process of making this movement. But it's fun. Your puppy will love it. Give it a try.

Click and give a treat every time your puppy's head moves towards you. He will soon make eye contact. Now you can use the watch me command and click and offer a treat when he looks at you.

You begin by teaching your puppy the meaning of the click. Use treats that are yummy to a dog – pea-size pieces of chicken, sausage or hard cheese (not slices wrapped in plastic). Use a room or area that is without distractions. Don't give any commands. Stand close to your dog, click the clicker, then give the puppy a treat. Repeat this four or five times and in different parts of the room or lawn. The next step is to click and delay the treat a few seconds. When the puppy alerts to the sound of the clicker, you're ready to begin shaping a behaviour.

Knowing a few of the basics will help you to get started. **Click *during* the desired movement.** *The timing of the click is crucial.* Your puppy will stop what he's doing when he hears the click, and that's okay. The click ends the behaviour. Give the treat after you click. You can lure your puppy into a position or motion by using hand or body movements, but don't push, pull or adjust with your hands. If you must have a leash on for safety reasons, loop it in your belt. Don't let it pull or restrict the puppy in any way. Keep the sessions short – no longer than five minutes.

Now choose a behaviour you want to teach, such as looking at you. When your puppy turns his head towards you even a little bit (make a movement if necessary), click and treat. Every time he moves his head a little bit farther in the direction you want, click and treat. In your next session, review by clicking any partial movements of his head, and give a bonus of several treats when he looks at you. When your puppy is confident at looking at you, add the command 'watch me', or whatever your command is, then click and treat. The next step is to click and treat randomly, not every time.

For the sit command, perhaps you have already taught your puppy by using a treat at his nose. Do that and click and treat as he sits. Wait until the puppy is performing the sit without the lure of your hand before you use the sit command. Or just watch for your puppy's rump to get closer to the ground before you click and treat. When he does the complete sit, you can add the command.

Karen Pryor suggests that you 'catch' cute behaviours when you are with your puppy, such as cocking the head or holding up a paw. You can click for a variety of different behaviours without confusing your dog. If you have two dogs, train them separately. Click for good behaviour. If your puppy jumps on people, don't give him any goodies unless he's sitting or has his feet on the floor. Then click and treat. If your dog barks, click and treat when he stops and is silent. When walking, click and treat when the leash is slack.

This is positive reinforcement (operant conditioning). In the traditional dog-training use of operant conditioning, the method in this book, you use your

Click and reward when the puppy's back legs bend.

After the puppy sits regularly, give the command to sit, then click and reward when he responds correctly.

voice and treats. Clicker training uses a sound (click) and a treat. The advantage of the clicker is the timing of the click, which is very precise and tells the dog which body movement you want. The more complex the command, the more types of movement you will need to click. For this, you need a teacher or a good book and a video. Use no corrections when you are clicker training. That will disrupt the puppy's attitude and perhaps lose the puppy's confidence in the clicker process.

Clicker training is another avenue of communication between you and your puppy. Find out more about it and proceed to enjoy working with your puppy in a most rewarding way.

Then Versus Now

In these high-tech times, the original job of most breeds has changed, but whatever a dog was bred for originally is still in his instincts, still a part of his natural abilities. Even though most dogs don't have an opportunity to do what they were bred for, they still need a job. The dog's job today is to be a companion to his people.

The people in the family pack can help the dog adjust to his new job. Most dogs adjust easily to being a companion because the dog is the most domesticated of all the animals, including the cat, and has bonded to humans for longer than memory. Dogs accept their people, recognise different moods, seem to know when they're needed for a hug or a long walk. Interacting with family members is the most important job a dog can have.

Amidst all the rapid changes of life in the twenty-first century, you will know the enduring joy of a loving partnership with your dog.

When your puppy obeys a command like sit, down or come, he's working with you. When he goes with you to take out the rubbish or do other chores around the house, he's working with you. When he obeys the rules of the house, waits for permission to go outdoors and greets visitors without jumping on them, he's working with you.

It is our responsibility, as leaders of the dog's family pack, to learn about our dog's natural instincts and talents. When we understand better what makes dogs tick, we can relate to them in ways that keep both people and dogs happy. Because the instincts that have been bred into various breeds are what cause dogs to behave as they do, training your puppy well is critically important to his well-being.

Dogs can no longer roam freely, trotting to the park with the children, following them as they move on to other pursuits, wandering back home to cool off in a patch of shade and visiting a few dog friends on the way.

No, the life of the dog is now much more formal and controlled. Because of this – because your dog no longer has the luxury of exercising his natural dog behaviour, expending energy whenever his energy level is high and socialising with his own subculture of friends – you owe him a lot. You owe him as good a life as you can give him. You owe him play time and learning time so that you can live together in mutual trust, joy and respect.

CHAPTER 13

The Second Six Months

There comes a day when you wonder what's wrong. Your puppy won't pay attention to you. In fact, he seems to be going out of his way to oppose you. Well, nothing's wrong — it's just one of the difficult times that a puppy goes through (difficult for you, but not for him). At six to seven months of age, and again around 12 months, your dog will challenge your leadership in the sense that he'll ignore you. This is a very normal thing for your puppy to do, so don't get upset. Tell him that you know what he's doing and that you're still the boss.

This is a transition age beyond puppyhood but prior to maturity. It's called adolescence, and it begins earlier in some puppies and later in others. Hormones are surging during these months. If your male puppy hasn't been neutered, he's becoming more intense and excitable about investigating everything in his environment. If a female hasn't been spayed, she may exhibit behaviours such as silliness and may not respond to commands that she knows. This can occur just before she comes into oestrus as well as during that period of time. Being spayed or neutered will not change your dog's personality, and it will make him or her a companion that is much easier to live with.

*Puppies appear to learn quickly —
but then it takes a long time for them to
acquire the confidence to perform consistently.*

During these months, the best approach with your puppy is to keep training the basic commands and using these commands to enforce your good behaviour policy. An obedience class is an excellent idea, because it puts you on a routine with weekly goals. Your young dog will learn to respond to you even with the distraction of other dogs. But applying these commands to help your dog maintain good manners at home is up to you.

PHOTO © ROBERT AND EUNICE PEARCY

Running, playing and retrieving help your puppy to get plenty of exercise, a big factor in good behaviour.

More Exercise, Less Freedom

Your adolescent will be much calmer to live with if he gets enough exercise. Play some running games. Form an imaginary square or triangle with friends or family, one person standing at each corner. All have treats and take turns calling your dog, waving their arms to get his attention. Once your dog figures out that everyone has a treat, he'll quickly learn to go to whoever is calling him. The person who has him holds the leash until he is called. If your dog runs off before he learns to go to whoever calls him, put him on a long line. If the treats are yummy enough, he'll soon learn. Retrieving is another running game. Make it fun. If your dog doesn't return, put a long line on him. Give him a treat when he gets back to you. You can stop the treat when he learns the game. Take him on short jogs, stopping or slowing fairly often.

Games to Play

Sniffing is a dog's way of learning about the world he lives in. Your puppy needs to do this. It's part of being a dog. Taking a dog jogging might exercise him, but without stopping at appropriate places and taking time to let him sniff around, you've given him nothing to do that is a part of the dog's world. You can do him a favour by taking him on leash to the park or around the neighbourhood. (Remember your plastic bag to clean up after your dog.) If it's a slow walk because he finds something to sniff, be patient. Then tell him it's time to move on. This is your gift to keep him relaxed in the human world. Whenever it's

PHOTO © ROBERT AND EUNICE PEARCY

Swimming is another good exercise.

possible, take him with you to a different place and let him sniff. This would imitate hunting in a different area.

At home you can play the **'find it' game.** Use the stay command or have a friend hold the leash, or tie it to a chair leg. Hide a biscuit or a toy. Let your dog watch you the first few times. Walk back to him, release him and tell him to find it. Help him if necessary until he reaches the point where he doesn't need to watch you hide it. Stand close to the place and point. If he begins to lose interest, clap your hands to get him excited. Praise him vigorously when he finds the object.

Get in front of your puppy. **Bounce a ball** so that it comes down close to him. He soon will learn to **catch it in midair.** When you begin, stay just a short distance away and bounce it so it will not go too far over his head. If you bounce it too hard, it will go too high and be difficult for him to keep track of and catch.

Play **hide and seek.** Even though this is a fun game, don't expect him to know how to play without some practice first. Have a friend hold his leash or distract him while you go out of the room or behind a piece of furniture when he isn't looking. Call him with the come command. Repeat 'come'. Make some noise. If you're behind a piece of furniture, pat the floor. If someone else is in the room, she can direct your puppy towards you. As soon as he stumbles into you, give a treat and lots of praise. You can gradually go farther away when you hide. You and your puppy will love this game. But if you go too far – such as into one room and through a door into another room – before he understands the game, it won't be fun for him anymore and he'll stop looking for you.

Let your puppy **retrieve**. Some dogs are 'born chasing a ball'; others have to learn what fun it is. Get your puppy excited by waving the ball in front of his nose. Toss it a short distance. If he sniffs or touches it with his nose, use lots of praise. Repeat only once or twice. Play this way each day until he picks up the ball.

If he begins to grab the ball and run off with it, tie to his collar a 6–9 m (20–30 ft) cord that won't hurt your hand. Don't wrap the line around your hand. You might get pulled down on the ground. If the ball rolls farther than the length of the line, drop the line, and then run after it and pick it up or stand on it. The purpose of the line is to keep your dog from running farther away. Talk to him. Try running in the opposite direction to see if he will follow you. Whenever the line gets a little bit loose, gather it in until you've folded the looseness in your hand. Don't pull him in like a fish, because he won't learn anything that way.

When he finally gets to you, take a treat from your pocket. If he drops the ball on his way back to you because he's in a hurry for a treat, don't scold him. You're teaching him to return to you. After he learns that, you won't give him a treat unless he brings the ball with him. These games and commands can help your dog learn to live more calmly with you.

Keeping Control

To keep your maturing puppy from getting into destructive mischief, keep him with you or in a crate for two to three hours, or in a pen or fenced garden with a dog house. This isn't cruel. It would be a lot more cruel if he kept destroying things and you took him to the animal shelter.

Your puppy should be with you whenever you're at home. Use your leash in the house if necessary. Hopefully, he learned 'place' when he was younger. If not, teach him now. He can also lie beside you. This will take repetition and patience until he learns that he can't wander off. That's why you keep the leash on him. Keep your foot on it, or put the leash through your belt loop.

Teach your dog 'leave it' so you have control over his grabbing and running. Put several items he's not allowed to have, such as a chocolate biscuit, on the floor. When he reaches for it as you walk past, turn quickly with a brisk leash pull and say 'leave it'. Very soon he will walk past, ignoring the items and practically hugging your leg. You will need to repeat this periodically to reinforce 'leave it'.

Work diligently to teach your young dog how to behave when friends come. He is vigorous and excited, and you can't expect him to automatically be a good dog unless you teach him how to act. We can't tell you how many repetitions that will take. It depends on your consistency and your dog's level of excitability. Hopefully, you have already taught the sit command very thoroughly. If not, get busy.

Use the Basic Commands to Control Behaviour

You need an attitude of determination and a will to be consistent with your training regimen. You must insist on your dog learning good behaviour when friends arrive, and on his using good door behaviour when he goes in and out. You must expect your dog to respond to you and to be controlled when you're out walking and other people approach. This is where determination and consistency come in. You must insist on good behaviour (without losing patience and saying, 'Oh, it's hopeless'), and you must use the same procedure (consistency) each time you correct a behaviour. If you can manage these two factors, you will be amazed that your dog's behaviour actually does improve.

Reinforce Basic Commands

The sit command is one that you will use for control in any situation. It's an excellent way to discipline your dog in the sense that it stops his bad behaviour (he can't jump or run or even bark much if he's on a sit stay), and it puts you in control and gains your dog's respect.

Practise your skills while out on walks and you will find yourself with a delightful, well-mannered companion.

To make certain that your dog understands 'sit' to mean 'sit now', do random sits. Walk him a few steps, not on a heel command but on a 'let's go', and give him the sit command. If he ignores you, put your right hand on the leash near the collar and your left hand across his back just in front of his hind legs. Pull up on the leash, and squeeze down and back with the thumb and third finger of your left hand. Repeat the 'sit' as you sit him. Always be ready to use both hands to sit your dog if he doesn't respond to your command immediately. You can progress to using only the leash, tugged straight up, on the sit. Then he should begin responding to the sit without any cues from you. But always be ready to show him that you're alert and in control and that you will correct him instantly whenever he ignores your command.

Use this same approach when you're reviewing the other commands that your dog knows. You have to concentrate as much or more than you expect your dog to. The more you concentrate on what you're doing, the better your timing will be for a leash or a voice correction if your dog doesn't respond properly.

Keep your puppy with you as much as possible. Notice that the dog's owner is sitting on the leash.

Left: Your puppy should be on a leash as you answer the doorbell.
Right: Ask your puppy to sit while he is greeted by the visitor. If your puppy needs several commands before he settles down, just stay with it until he obeys.

Insist on Good Manners

Now that your dog really understands the sit command, you can use it to teach good manners. If your dog jumps at people or at other dogs when he's out walking with you, tell him 'no', give him a pop on the leash to get him back to you, and say 'sit'! Let him sit there for several seconds, and get eye contact with a 'watch me'. At that point, you can tell him that he's a good dog and continue walking. Sometimes you will give your dog a sit command before a person gets close. Your dog can learn to sit there without leaping up until you give permission for him to move.

Greeting Visitors at the Front Door

The sit command is excellent for teaching good manners at your front door. Some dogs are easy to teach to sit while the door is opened, but if your dog has developed a bad habit of barking and jumping and in general being out of control when someone comes to the door, you might need the reinforcement of a squirt bottle with a dilution of vinegar and water (approximately one to six) ready to use. Use this only until your dog begins to understand what's expected.

Enlist some friends to help you by ringing your doorbell and then waiting patiently to enter while you work with your dog. After the first few times, you won't need a leash for this, because your dog will learn more quickly when he must be totally responsible for his own actions without being tugged and pulled on a leash.

When your dog becomes very excited and is barking at the door, give a sit command. He will probably keep barking because he's so excited. Repeat the sit command, and squirt at his lips with the vinegar water. Keep repeating the sit command until your dog sits. You might be some distance away from the door by now because your dog will keep moving around, but just keep moving with him. When he is finally sitting and not barking, quietly tell him that he's a good dog. After your friends come through the door, you can release your dog from his sit. If he wants to jump up, insist that he sit again. Once you and your dog understand this procedure at the door, the dog will be more relaxed (as will you) and will sit without all the jumping around, and without being squirted with vinegar water.

Another good use of the sit command is to have your dog on leash and ask him to wait while you open the door. Step outside the door and then call your dog to you. The same procedure applies when you come back in. This reminds your dog of who's in control, and it keeps him from bolting out of the door or knocking you over to be the first one into the house.

The sit command can also be used if your dog is playing around out of reach and won't come to you. Keep saying 'sit-sit-sit', pointing your finger and staring at him. Follow him wherever he wiggles or moves to, and you will eventually get a sit from him. Now go to him and tell him that he's a good dog because he sat. This procedure reinforces the come command when your dog is feeling his independence.

When you train off leash and your dog doesn't come on command, walk close, say 'come' and run away. After a few steps, turn and face him. Guide with hand movements and your voice so that he will come and sit in front of you. Praise with a treat.

If your dog ignores the come command, runs playfully and bumps you, stop training immediately. Walk away and ignore him. This teaches him that he gets no attention for doing this – it won't be fun any more and he will stop.

The Come

A long line is essential now so that you are in control and can make your dog come to you even if he doesn't want to. After several weeks of using a long line or Flexi-Lead and rewarding him for coming and checking in with you, your dog should be reliable off leash in safe fields or greenbelt areas. One of our students, Jim, was considering renting an electronic collar because his Standard Schnauzer needed exercise but kept running off. We discussed the pros and cons; two weeks later he phoned and said that he didn't need the remote-control collar – cheese had done the job. Keep calling your dog to you, give a reward, and let him run off again – but don't let him get more than 9 m (30 ft) away before calling him.

The Down Stay

Using this command allows your dog to be with the family at times when he would otherwise be a nuisance. Fix him a special place to stay when you're eating or have friends visiting. Make his place comfortable for him. Give a down command and a stay command. Keep the stay short, only a minute or two. Extend it gradually. Every time he gets up, put him back down. You may have to repeat this often at first, but if you're consistent he'll learn quickly. Give a treat when you release him.

Walking on the Leash

When you walk your dog in a park, or any public area, respect the other people who also use the park. Take some plastic sandwich bags with you. When your dog defecates, put a plastic bag on your hand like a mitten, pick up the faeces

Well-socialised dogs are a joy to take walking. These two young dogs are six and 11 months old.

Every time your dog starts to drag you on the leash, call him to you.

Reward him for coming, then continue your walk.

and pull the bag off so that the pile you picked up is now inside the bag. Carry a small paper bag with you to keep the plastic bag in until you reach a litter bin. If dog owners all did this, they would be more welcome in public areas.

Use the come command when your dog is pulling too hard on the leash. Call your dog, walk backwards a few steps, and reward him when he gets to you. Now walk forwards again and let him move along beside you. Repeat calling him to you whenever he pulls on the leash. Using a Flexi-Lead takes a lot of pressure off your arms and shoulders and gives the dog more freedom and distance to exercise. If you walk where you meet numerous people and their dogs, however, a leash offers much more control.

Behavioural Traits

Your puppy's personality will continue to develop during the next few months. Some behavioural traits don't become strongly developed until the dog is a year old or more. Traits such as stubbornness and extreme independence were undoubtedly hinted at during puppyhood but were very easy to ignore because 'he was only a puppy', or because it hadn't become a problem yet. With puppy training, you probably nipped many problems in the bud before they became deeply entrenched. As the dog matures, however, you must continue to assert your role of leadership.

Other behavioural problems, such as barking or a lapse in house-training, can be caused by stress or by a change in the daily home routine. Such stresses might include a stay in a boarding kennel or a schedule change by a member of the family who had previously been at home and then went back to school or work.

Some behavioural traits aren't very noticeable until the dog reaches sexual maturity, and then they can become obvious problems requiring attention. Roaming and overprotectiveness are some examples. The roaming dog must not have the opportunity to wander. He must be confined in a garden or house, or be under your total control when he's outside his home.

Some dogs have a genetic disposition towards protectiveness, and sexual maturity accentuates it. Some dogs will just naturally try an aggressive reaction in certain circumstances, and when they find out that you won't permit it, they should cease that type of behaviour. When you are walking your dog on a leash, any demonstration of growling or lip curling must immediately be stopped. An instant 'no', accompanied by an abrupt turn in the opposite direction for a few steps, and then followed by a 'sit' and a 'watch me' should work. Tell him that you won't permit such behaviour. You can now turn back to where you were. If he behaves, tell him that he's a good dog.

Territoriality

Almost all dogs have a sense of territory. Unless a dog has been totally forbidden to do so, he will automatically announce the arrival of someone at the door or on the property. Some dogs have stronger-than-average senses of territory and enlarge their area to include the route of their regular walks through the neighbourhood. An aggressive male dog could become a problem because of trying to fight other males that are intruding on 'his' street or pavement. The degree of a dog's protective actions is based on the relationship that you have established with him. If you have let him have his own way, the protectiveness will begin to show at this age. The puppy will begin to put himself in the role of pack leader. This means that if he has tendencies towards overprotectiveness, he will growl if someone comes near his food bowl.

Some people think that they want a guard dog and should allow this kind of behaviour. This is not correct. It isn't necessary to encourage aggressive actions in order to have a dog that barks and warns you of strangers. Most dogs will automatically do this. A dog that is not controllable is dangerous to have around. Now is the time to get involved with a formal training programme and get your relationship back on track.

Separation Anxiety

This is diagnosed in dogs that, when left at home alone, engage in disruptive behaviours such as barking, howling, chewing, digging and elimination. It's not disobedience. It's a dog in distress, a dog that is well behaved when you're at home but becomes intensely stressed when you leave. You might have taught your puppy to stay at home alone as discussed in Chapter 11, but now, several months later, the problem arises and you wonder what you can do about it. Punishment is inappropriate and not effective. You cannot put your dog in a crate when dealing with separation anxiety. It only intensifies his anxiety to the extent of damaging the crate or breaking its door.

Most anxiety behaviours occur during the first five to ten minutes after you leave home. There are several things you can do to help your dog relax during this time. One of these is to practise graduated departures, perhaps taking a weekend to work on this. Some dogs begin their stress behaviours instantly, so start by timing your absence for just a few seconds and then return. We've worked with dogs where we began simply by closing the door and opening it again. Work up to a minute, then two minutes, back to one minute, then three. Work up to five minutes and, when your dog appears calm at your return, begin to work for longer times, periodically going back to two or three minutes.

Use the same cue words each time you leave, such as, 'See you soon. Be a good dog'. It doesn't matter what words you say as long as they're always the same and spoken in a neutral voice. Each time you depart, give your dog a chew toy that is stuffed with biscuits, and a hollow, sterilised bone with some cheese in it. These will keep your puppy busy for the first few minutes. If you've been leaving the radio on during your absence, change to using the television.

Think about your actions just before you leave the house. Practise your routine, leave, then return right away. You can do this several times during a day but not during the timed departures. For example, put your coat on, reach for your handbag or car keys and whatever else you do, and then leave. Your goal is to eliminate stress when your dog watches these activities by making it a common event after which you return.

If these routines aren't changing the behaviour, seek professional help. Most vets are familiar with this problem and will know if there is a medication that will help your dog deal with the initial anxiety. Then you can begin again with the procedures discussed above.

Communication

By now you undoubtedly have learnt a great deal about communicating with your puppy. Dogs learn a vocabulary of 100 words or more. They know the meaning of outside, walk, supper, car, biscuit, sit, stay and many other words. Unfortunately, we can become so intent on what we want to say to our dog that we forget to listen to what the dog has to say. Continue to watch for the signals your dog is sending (as explained in Chapter 10). Have you had the wonderful experience of catching a look of surprise or a startled expression on your dog's face? (They're similar but not identical.) The eyes get big – you know exactly what's being communicated by the shape of the mouth and facial muscles. But these are fleeting signals. If you aren't aware, you'll miss them. Think about the context of the signal – what you are doing, what is going on at that moment. The more you observe your dog's signals, the better you will understand him.

Sexual Maturity

The indication that the female has reached sexual maturity is the onset of oestrus, commonly called the heat period. This is not an indication of physical or behavioural maturity, because there is still much growth yet to occur in these areas. There is an apparent correlation between breed size and the onset of the first oestrus. It generally occurs at six to eight months for females less than 14 kg (30 lb), at eight to ten months for females 14–27 kg (30–60 lb), and at ten to 15 months for breeds greater than 27 kg (60 lb). However, there are always individual differences in these groups. The total length of the heat period lasts about three weeks.

PHOTO © JUDITH STROM

Your early training is paying off. When your puppy gets excited, go back to basics.

The male, at some time during the last half of the first year, will begin to lift his leg to urinate. This is usually viewed as a mark of the sexually maturing male and can begin anywhere from five to 12 months, or even later. Sexual maturity often brings on an increased attitude of protectiveness and an intense interest in other dogs. As we have already stated, you may have to take specific steps to reinforce your position as pack leader.

After the male reaches the age where he is leg-lifting, he might begin to do it to excess. Leg-lifting is the manner in which a male marks his territory. Many people think that they must allow their dog to stop at every blade of grass if that is what the dog wants. Excessive leg-lifting is often a demonstration that the dog has a strong tendency towards being the pack leader, and this is one way of telling you that he's taking over the job. Leg-lifting to such an excess isn't necessary. It isn't pleasant to take a dog for a walk if he's constantly stopping to lift his leg. Therefore, during your walk, have a couple of stops where he can lift his leg several times. Then continue the walk at a brisk pace on your terms. The routine can be adjusted to fit the involved individuals as long as the dog gets his bladder empty and as long as you remain in charge.

Some males have the irritating habit of lifting their leg in the house, often in one particular room or on certain pieces of furniture. The smaller breeds seem to be more persistent in this activity than the large breeds. If your dog has a favourite area, keep it cleaned and deodorised. Dogs will naturally mark a spot that has been used previously. Another possible reason for this behaviour is that your dog considers the house to be his territory (you just happen to live there and provide food). An obedience course can help you and your dog understand your relationship with each other. If your dog persists in this behaviour, neutering is recommended.

Undesirable Behaviours

This is the age when young males begin to display behaviours that you might find objectionable. Male hormones surge to a peak of nine times normal and then level back down again, which is one reason why this is a period of behavioural changes. Some males go through a phase of continually trying to mount other dogs. This is part of the maturing process and is in the category of play and trying new behavioural activities (which doesn't mean that you have to allow it to go on and on). Distraction is sufficient discipline for most dogs. If your young male has exceptional qualities and is being considered for breeding stock, it's best not to severely discipline the dog, because this could affect his breeding desire in the future. When your dog begins to mount another dog, call him to you or use your leash or hand on his collar to move him away. Then you can distract him, praise his attention to you and give him a sit command with a piece of biscuit for a reward. (Don't you always have a few biscuits in your pocket when you take a walk or even when you are just hanging around the house?)

Another disturbing behaviour is when your dog mounts a person's leg or any other object to which the dog takes a fancy. Use the off command for your correction. Insist that the dog stop. Then give him a sit command and praise him when he obeys your command and his attention is on you.

With consistent correction, followed by a command such as sit (which is a behaviour that you can praise), many dogs will keep these behaviours to a minimum. For the dog that continues to be extreme in mounting other dogs or human legs, the solution is either to neuter the dog or to remove the dog from the stimulus of people or other dogs when he can't otherwise be controlled. A drug treatment is available, and your vet can be consulted about this, as well as about any potential side effects it may have.

Spaying and Neutering

One of the ways in which dogs can be helped to adjust to an urban or suburban environment is to spay or neuter them. This is not mistreating the dog or depriving him of natural feelings that are his 'right'. If the hormones don't send the message to the brain, the dog doesn't know what he's missing. In fact, it makes his life more pleasant because it removes some of the behavioural traits which people find it difficult to live with.

Don't consider keeping your male or female for breeding unless he or she is an outstanding individual in the breed and you are willing to spend all the time necessary to learn what must be learnt before you can become a conscientious breeder. In addition, be willing to volunteer your time and effort to work in your community with the pet overpopulation problem. Many breeds have rescue societies that take a dog of their breed out of the shelter, do any training that needs doing and then find him a home.

The Female. There is no reason for your female to have one heat period before she is spayed. If you would like to avoid the problem of confining her while she's in heat, try to time the operation before her first heat period. If she isn't spayed until after her heat period, it's a good idea to wait for about two months, because it takes this long for the progesterone level to decline completely. If progesterone secretion is suddenly stopped, nervousness or irritability may occur for a time. This can be offset, however, by having your vet administer a long-acting progestin. The behaviour of the bitch remains normal after the spay operation, because this is the natural condition of the female between heat periods. A common myth about spaying is that the bitch becomes fat and lazy. If these conditions should occur, it's a result of overfeeding and under-exercising.

The Male. Neutering does not change the dog's masculine appearance, because he will still acquire his secondary sex characteristics regardless of his age when the procedure is done; nor does neutering affect hunting ability or watch-dog behaviour. There are individual differences in how it affects other behaviours. Some differences are probably a result of the environment, but many are due to breed and genetics. Roaming showed the greatest degree of change, with more than 90 per cent of the dogs having either a rapid or gradual decline. This is probably a result of the lessening in sexual drive. Fighting with other male dogs declined rapidly in 40 per cent of the dogs and gradually in 22 per cent. About 50 per cent showed a decline in urine-marking in the house. The act of mounting dropped rapidly in about one-third of the dogs studied and gradually declined in another one-third. Much of this decline was in mounting people, so neutering appeared to be a good way to reduce this problem.

There doesn't appear to be any proven difference in effect if this is done before puberty or in the adult dog. In fact, some humane shelters and some breeders are neutering their puppies by four months of age before they are placed in their new homes. Recent studies have shown no ill effects. And as is true with the female spay operation, there is no basis for the idea that neutered dogs become fat and lazy.

The Good Citizen Dog Scheme

The Kennel Club promotes the Good Citizen Dog Scheme. The scheme is run at many local clubs and incorporates a Bronze, Silver and Gold award. For each level the dogs are tested singly or in groups by an examiner. The dog completes a series of tests and the examiner awards a pass or else says that 'the dog is not ready'.

To receive the Bronze Award, the handler and dog must pass ten tests. First, the handler must have with her some form of 'poop scoop' and all dogs must wear a collar and identification tag complying with the law. The handler must be able to put on and take off the collar and leash safely. The handler and dog should be able to walk for approximately 30 paces, including some turns, without the dog pulling forward or back. Handler and dog should be able to walk through a gate or doorway under control and on a lead, as well as among people, dogs and distractions. When instructed to do so, the dog should remain in place when the handler moves away for one minute. The handler should be able to groom a dog, as well as be able to examine the dog's mouth, teeth, throat, eyes, ears, stomach, tail and feet without any signs of struggle or concern from the dog. The dog should return to the handler from a short distance away when instructed to do so. Finally, the handler has to be able to answer a number of questions about the responsibility and care of a dog.

The Silver Award builds on the skills learned in the Bronze Award but increases the level of difficulty. Only dogs that already have a Bronze Award can go on to the Silver Award. The Gold Award develops more advanced training skills and introduces new concepts such as stopping the dog in an emergency situation and sending the dog to bed, not as a punishment but as another form of control.

144 Chapter 13 • The Second Six Months

These awards are well worth working towards as you continue to train and socialise your growing puppy. You will be delighted by the handsome certificate and rosette you receive for each level.

For more information about the Good Citizen Dog Scheme look up the website of the Kennel Club, **www.thekennelclub.org.uk**, or contact the Kennel Club by phone on 0870 606 6750, or by fax on 020 7518 1058.

You and your dog can earn these certificates. Insist on good manners at home. The sit and down commands are good for this. Insist on good manners when you're out walking, meeting other people and dogs, and this will all come about. Receiving each certificate will give you a great feeling and mark a milestone for you and your dog working as a team.

Don't Worry - Have Fun!

During much of this chapter, we've been looking at worst-case scenarios. We certainly don't want to leave you with a dismal attitude concerning this age span of your puppy's growth. It's a fun age, and if you are so inclined this is the time to start working on the performance event of your choice. Training for obedience, agility, tracking, herding, frisbee and many other performance events can begin in earnest when your puppy is between six and 18 months of age. The point we want to make here is that most bad behaviours can be squelched immediately if you get at them as soon as they occur.

If we didn't think that the rewards would be vastly greater than your training efforts, we wouldn't have written the book.

Good luck – and let us know how things turn out.

CHAPTER 14

Puppy Temperament Training

Authors' Note

To put puppy testing in proper perspective, it is important to note that it is one of the tools to use in evaluating a puppy's temperament. The other tools are the breeder's continuing observation of each puppy's behaviour throughout the first seven weeks, not only in the litter but also when separated and spending time with a person, and a knowledge of the behavioural factors in that particular breed and those particular bloodlines. The puppy buyer should not get hung up on the scoring but realise it's an indication of the puppy's socialisation needs in his new home. Dominance, shyness and over-excitability are readily identifiable general traits in some dogs that need special placement in homes that are willing to work with these personalities.

Many of you might select your puppy without using the test we have here. We discuss this type of puppy selection in Chapter 1 and give you steps to help you to evaluate the personalities of the puppies from which you are choosing.

The puppy buyer should not get hung up on temperament testing scoring but realise it's an indication of the puppy's socialisation needs in his new home.

The Temperament Test

Whether you use the more general selection process or the puppy temperament test that follows, the most important personality traits you will evaluate are willingness to please and willingness to forgive. Willingness to please is noted in the Come, the Following and the Retrieving tests. Willingness to forgive is shown in the Restraint, the Touch and the Social Dominance tests.

It's easy and fun to administer puppy tests, but it's also easy to form snap judgements as a result of the tests. A puppy test is an indication of the puppy's natural attitude towards people and a relative measure of the puppy's submissiveness and aggressiveness. As such, it's a guide to what type of home and what kind of training will work best. It's not a permanent labelling of the puppy's adult personality. One reason for this is that environment plays such a large part in the development of a dog's personality.

Refrain from making snap judgements about a puppy's personality from test results. It's merely a guide for how best to work with your dog's abilities and attitude.

William Campbell was one of the first to develop this series of puppy tests, which give a consistent overall picture of a puppy's basic emotional behaviour. Wendy Volhard and Gail Tamases Fisher have contributed greatly to the widespread use of what they term 'puppy aptitude testing'. Our score sheet is modelled after theirs and lists the reactions we have found to be fairly common. The analysis sheet is a guide to interpreting the results of the testing and incorporates our interpretations of scoring based on observations of the testing we have done.

Breeders who use puppy testing tend to develop a sharp eye from experience. They become familiar with the behavioural tendencies of their bloodlines and with how certain reactions will develop later in adult dogs. They also can see certain behavioural qualities that are not testable, such as that extra spark of intelligence or charisma. Some puppies will have a reaction not listed on the score sheet. For example, a puppy will not be shy but will be content to observe and quietly do what is indicated, but in his own time. This is probably an indication of a slightly more than average independence, or possibly it points to an easy-going, quiet disposition. The puppy can be retested another day to make certain he wasn't tired at the first test.

Many breeders prefer to conduct the test by scoring each puppy while another person does the actual testing. This gives the breeder an overall view of the behaviour of the litter, and this information can be helpful when discussing selection with potential new owners. The breeder might be surprised to discover that a puppy's test score can be quite different from what his litter behaviour indicated. A puppy that is very quiet, even to the extent of being picked on by the others, can score as an outgoing, people-oriented puppy. The reverse can also be true. An assertive puppy in the litter might hesitate in association with a new person. Observation of the litter behaviour with the other puppies can sometimes give a false impression of the puppy's innate desire to please and to adjust to people, so it's always advisable for a breeder to puppy-test a litter even though it sometimes seems unnecessary.

Guidelines for Testing

Seven weeks of age is the optimum age for testing. The puppy has the brain waves of an adult dog but is not affected to any degree by experience and learning. Therefore, the tests reveal the puppy's basic individual temperament. The object is to test each puppy in the same environment and at the same level of activity. The tests should be administered by a person unknown to the puppies and conducted in a room or area that is new to them. These two factors are the means of introducing a puppy's reaction to a new person and a new environment into the testing. The place of the testing should be away from the noise of the litter and with as few distractions as possible. The time of the testing should be during one of the play times in the puppies' daily schedule, but not immediately after mealtime. If any of the puppies fall asleep, give them time to run around and wake up first. Each puppy, when taken from the litter, should be given a couple of minutes to urinate or defecate before being taken to the tester. During each of the test activities, the tester can use voice and hand motions.

Performing the Tests

Come (Social Attraction)

The breeder or helper carries the puppy and places him on the floor or grass 1.2 m (4ft) in front of the kneeling tester. She stands for a second, then leaves. (If the puppy follows the helper, he is placed again.) As soon as the puppy is on the floor, the tester gets the puppy's attention using a soft voice and hands and patting the floor if necessary. The tester strokes the puppy a few seconds and the observer notes the actions of the puppy – jumping on the tester, climbing on her lap, grabbing the jersey, running off or quietly accepting the stroking. If the puppy doesn't come, the tester reaches out with her hand, wiggling her fingers and quietly coaxing the puppy. You want the puppy to experience success, but the scoring will still be a 'no-come'.

Following

The tester slowly stands close to the puppy, encouraging the puppy with her voice and her hand patting her leg, to follow. The puppy might jump and run alongside, getting in the way, or walk with his tail down, or leave and go somewhere else. Staying at your side for two or three steps constitutes a following.

Restraint

This test is immediately followed by the Forgiveness test. For the restraint, the tester, kneeling, gently rolls the puppy over on his back, keeping one hand on its chest. The pressure is just enough to keep the puppy from getting up. The tester maintains a neutral, pleasant expression for 30 seconds, with no talking, and notices if the puppy gives her any eye contact. This test and the Forgiveness test are the most important ones for evaluating the type of home that is best for the puppy. The best puppy for the average home is the one that shows little dominance and that reacts without fear (middle range).

Forgiveness (Social Dominance)

As soon as the puppy is on his feet, the tester sits him at a 45-degree angle in front, using an arm or hand for a second to keep him in place. Then the tester strokes from head to tail, leaning down so

that her face is available to be licked. The tester can talk to the puppy. The

unforgiving puppy will turn his head away. This puppy will mature into a dog that will hold a grudge or will refuse to respond if the owner does something he doesn't like. The forgiving puppy will wash the face or gently lick or nuzzle the cheek with his nose. The independent puppy will walk away. The aggressive puppy will growl or nip the tester.

Elevation Dominance

This test shows the degree of accepting human dominance when the puppy has no control over the situation. The tester laces her fingers under the puppy and lifts until the puppy's feet are several centimetres off the floor. This position is maintained for 30 seconds with no talking. The relaxed puppy that just hangs there will, as an adult, accept conditions over which he has no control. The dominant puppy won't accept this position without a struggle. The shy puppy will freeze – this is a puppy that will have trouble adapting to new situations.

Retrieving

Retrieving a sheet of typing paper crumpled up into a ball is an indication of concentration and desire to please. This test is applicable to all breeds. It's more of a test of willingness to perform a task than of retrieving. The tester gets the puppy's attention by touching his lips with the balled paper and teasing him with it. The ball is tossed about 1 m (3 ft) away. If the puppy goes out to it, he demonstrates he can pay attention to an object. If he brings it back to you, he has a strong desire to please or to work with a person. Some puppies, even retrieving breeds, aren't interested in going out to the tossed paper ball. This isn't a mark against them. Retrieving is a game you can teach later. Look for the puppy's willingness to please in other areas of the testing.

Touch Sensitivity

This tests the puppy's sensitivity to pain. The tester either sits the puppy beside her or holds him in the crook of the arm. She then takes a front foot and puts pressure between the toes with the thumb and index finger. (This can also be performed by pinching an ear instead of a foot.) Squeezing with increasing pressure, the tester counts from one to ten. The pressure stops as soon as the puppy reacts, either by jerking away or biting or yipping. An overly sensitive puppy can't deal with the light pressure of the first or second count. The middle range indicates a dog that will respond readily to collar and leash training. The puppy whose count is in the top of the range isn't touch sensitive, and training will probably take more time and effort.

Sound Sensitivity

This test shows the puppy's reaction to a loud sound. When the puppy faces away, the tester hits a metal pan with a spoon. The puppy that notices the sound, locates it and perhaps walks towards it is very confident. The puppy that startles and recovers quickly is a very normal puppy. The puppy that runs away and tries to hide is very sound sensitive and shouldn't be placed in a noisy family or with someone who will be taking him to dog events or other events that are noisy. If the puppy has no reaction, try again. This might be an independent puppy or possibly one that is deaf if you have a breed in which this occurs.

Sight Sensitivity

This test allows the puppy to interact with a new object. The tester will pull a towel tied to a cord across the testing area. Playful interaction shows adaptability to new situations. The puppy that cowers or startles will have a tough time in new situations.

Energy Level

This category is another aid in matching the puppy to the prospective owner. The high-energy person won't be happy with a quiet puppy, and the person whose lifestyle is calm and whose exercise consists of a walk around the block won't be able to deal with a puppy that is always in motion.

Notes and Observations

Notes can be as important as the test scores. We can attest to the vital role of note-taking. One prospective puppy owner was looking for an assertive puppy that could take a lot of work and training but that also had a strong desire to please. She had the first pick of the litter and had narrowed the selection to two puppies with similar scores on the puppy test. However, her notes told her that Puppy One had come to the tester on the first Come test even though he was distracted by a frayed rug corner. Puppy Two needed three comes. Early records by the breeder showed that Puppy One was the only puppy that didn't cry when removed from the litter and put on a cement floor at three and a half weeks of age. He also was the most investi-

gative puppy with a rapidly wagging tail. This cinched the selection, but she needed the written notes to help her with her decision.

The puppy-testing session is an excellent opportunity for making general observations under conditions that are the same for all the puppies. What is each puppy's reaction to the tester and to the surroundings? Is he generally very curious and active, or is he hesitant? Does he whine? Write down all the observations. It's amazing how easy it is to forget the little details when observing several puppies.

For the potential owner, the breeder can point out the more cautious puppies from the more aggressive ones and can also casually incorporate the Come and the Follow tests into the visit. In the final analysis, the selection of a puppy is probably more emotional than logical. However, it's best to place the puppy in the home that fits his natural personality. Many future problems can be prevented this way. An assertive person will quickly lose patience with a quiet puppy, and a shy person will never be able to become the leader of a puppy with a dominant personality.

See chart on the following pages for charting individual test results >>

PUPPY ID   Litter   Tester

            Date   Age of Litter   Note-taker

COME (Social Attraction)

Place puppy in test area. From a short distance
away, the tester coaxes the puppy to come by
clapping hands gently and kneeling down. Tester
must coax in a direction away from the point where
the puppy entered the testing area.

Degree of social attraction,
confidence or dependence.

FOLLOWING

Tester stands up and walks away from the pup
in a normal manner. Make sure the puppy sees
the tester walk away.

Degree of following attraction.
Not following indicates
independence or fear.

RESTRAINT

Tester is on hands and knees. Gently roll
puppy onto back and hold with one hand
for a full 30 seconds.

Degree of dominant or
submissive tendency. How
puppy accepts stress when
socially/physically dominated.

FORGIVENESS

Tester is still kneeling. Sit puppy across your
front, slightly facing you. Give him a few seconds
to settle down, then gently stroke him and lean down
so face can be licked. Continue stroking until a
recognisable behaviour is established.

Degree of acceptance of social
dominance. Pup may try to
dominate by jumping and
nipping or may be independent
and walk away.

ELEVATION DOMINANCE

Tester is still kneeling. Pick up puppy, cradle
puppy under his belly, fingers interlaced, palms up
and elevate puppy to just off the ground.
Hold there for 30 seconds.

Degree of accepting
dominance while in a position
of no control.

RETRIEVING

Kneel beside puppy and attract his attention with
crumpled paper. When puppy shows interest and
is watching, toss the object 1 m (3 ft) in front
of puppy.

Degree of willingness to work
with a human. High correlation
between ability to retrieve and
successful guide dogs,
obedience dogs and field
trial dogs.

TOUCH SENSITIVITY

Take webbing of a front foot between your finger
and thumb. Press lightly, then increase firmly until
you get a response while you slowly count to ten.
Stop as soon as puppy pulls away. Repeat with ear.

Degree of sensitivity
to touch.

Came readily, tail up, jumped, barked, bit at hands.	1
Came readily, tail up, pawed, licked at hands.	2
Came readily, tail up.	3
Came readily, tail down.	4
Came hesitantly or no come, fearful.	5
Did not come at all, wandered and sniffed.	6
Followed readily, tail up, got underfoot, bit at feet.	1
Followed readily, tail up, got underfoot.	2
Followed readily, tail up.	3
Followed readily, tail down.	4
Huddled, would not move.	5
No follow or went away.	6
Struggled fiercely, flailed, bit.	1
Vigorously flailed, some eye contact.	2
Settled, struggled, settled with good eye contact.	3
Struggled, then settled with some eye contact.	4
No struggle – froze.	5
No struggle, strained to avoid eye contact.	6
Jumped, pawed, bit, growled.	1
Jumped, pawed.	2
Cuddled up to tester, licked face.	3
Squirmed, licked hands.	4
Rolled over, huddled.	5
Went away and stayed away.	6
Struggled fiercely, bit, growled.	1
Settled, then struggled.	2
No struggle, relaxed.	3
Struggled, then settled.	4
No struggle, froze.	5
No struggle, no eye contact.	6
Chased object, picked up and ran away.	1
Chased object, picked up and did not return.	2
Chased object, returned with it to tester.	3
Chased object and returned to tester without it.	4
Stayed with tester, worried.	5
Did not chase object.	6

Note number of counts before response:

TOE _____ EAR _____

SECOND SOCIAL DOMINANCE

Continue holding puppy in your arms until he
either forgives by licking your cheek or
get down.

Degree of forgiveness.

SOUND SENSITIVITY

Place puppy in centre of area. Strike pan with a
large spoon a short distance behind the puppy.

Degree of sensitivity to
sound. May be a rudimentary
test for deafness.

SIGHT SENSITIVITY

Place puppy in centre of area; jerk a towel
tied to a string across the floor for
a short distance.

Degree of intelligent response
to a strange object.

ENERGY LEVEL

Note how active puppy is throughout the
testing.

❑ Jumped up all the time (*boing-boing*)
❑ Bouncy
❑ Relaxed
❑ Slow, quiet
❑ Little participation (the observer)
❑ No interest

Circle one of the following responses:

Puppy quickly forgave and licked.	Puppy snuggled, no kisses.	Slow, or no forgiving.

Listened, located sound, walked towards it barking.	1
Listened, located sound, showed curiosity, walked towards it.	2
Listened, located sound.	3
Listened, startled.	4
Cringed, backed off, hid.	5
Ignored sound, showed no curiosity.	6

Looked, attacked, bit.	1
Looked, grabbed, head shaking.	2
Looked, became curious.	3
Looked, tail tucked.	4
Ran away, hid.	5
Ignored it, no interest.	6

Analysis of Puppy Test

Mostly '5' responses. Shies away for no reason. Retest to verify. This puppy needs a low-stress environment.

Mostly '4' responses. A submissive but not shy puppy. Needs confidence building. Very trainable if not rushed. Easy to live with.

Mostly '3' responses, with some '4s'. Will be a happy dog. Good with children. Good for the inexperienced trainer. A family companion.

Mostly '3' responses, with some '2s'. Will fit into a family with older children. Very active and does best with obedience training.

Mostly '2' responses, with some '3s'. Outgoing and eager to please but needs a firm hand or will make a pest of himself.

Mostly '2' responses. Learns quickly and needs firm, consistent training. Does best with a person who has had training experience.

Mostly '1' responses. Very dominant. Not good with children. Untrustworthy around strangers. Needs special training with very experienced, dominant trainer. Can easily become aggressive.

Mostly '6' responses. Three '6s' in the first five tests is a very independent puppy. Doesn't require a lot of human attention. Training requires much repetition and patience.

Afterword

If you have helped your puppy to become a good family member, then you have in a small but nonetheless significant way contributed to helping the dog become a better and consequently more acceptable part of modern society. In this event, we would like to congratulate and thank you for joining the ranks of dog lovers in our combined effort to foster good interaction between human and dog, thereby enriching all our lives. If we had a much higher proportion of well-cared-for, well-behaved animals and fewer wandering garbage hounds, the dog's image with the growing army of the urban and rural disgruntled might not be so bad.

You've brought your puppy a long way and have developed a good communication system. Now you can look forward to a long and satisfying relationship. Although sometimes this relationship may take more effort than you had wanted to expend, at many other times, it will offer more rewards than you had dared to hope.

Index